Mt St Michel

Chinon

Poitiers

ANGLAIS

BOURGUIGNONS

ARMAGNACS
(France "libre")

Joan of Arc

MICHAEL MORPURGO

Joan of Arc
of Domrémy

ILLUSTRATED BY
MICHAEL FOREMAN

Hodder
Children's
Books

A division of Hodder Headline

For Christine Baker

The map at the beginning and end of this book is based on an
ancient French map from the period of Joan of Arc. The spellings
of place-names may not correspond with those names as
they appear on modern maps.

JOAN OF ARC
by Michael Morpurgo
Illustrated by Michael Foreman

British Library Cataloguing in Publication Data
A catalogue record of this book is available from the British Library

ISBN 0 340 73221 0

Text copyright © Michael Morpurgo 1998
Illustrations copyright © Michael Foreman 1998

First published in Great Britain in 1998 by
Pavilion Books, London House,
Great Eastern Wharf, London, SW11 4NQ

First paperback edition published in 2000 by
Hodder Children's Books,
a division of Hodder Headline,
338 Euston Road, London NW1 3BH

10 9 8 7 6 5 4 3 2 1

Printed in Hong Kong

Contents

❖

One Joan a Year

To begin with it was the picture. It was the picture that made it all happen – I am quite sure of it.

In the house where I grew up, in our old house in Montpellier, the picture always hung at the top of the stairs. Every time I went up to bed at night, there she'd be – Joan of Arc in her shining armour, holding her standard, with a shaft of light falling across her uplifted face. I would often gaze up at her and yearn to be serene and strong, just as she was. I wanted to have the same visionary, far-away look in my eyes, and the same hair-style too.

But I learned very early on that my father did not share my enthusiasm. He disliked the picture intensely, about as intensely as my mother loved it. Apparently it had hung in her house when she was a child. But I didn't like it just because my mother did. I had my own reasons, reasons I always kept to myself – until now.

*   *   *

My name is Eloise Hardy. I was seventeen last May. Something extraordinary has just happened to me, something so extraordinary that I feel I have to write it down. I want to remember all of it as it really happened, every moment of it, every word of it. Maybe, in the remembering of it, in the writing of it, I will begin to understand it better. I hope so.

One of my very earliest memories is of me standing in front of the full-length mirror in my mother's bedroom, a red tablecloth over my shoulders for a cloak, a broom with a towel tied to it for my standard. I would contrive to strike my saintliest pose. I once wrote out every adjective I could think of that described her perfectly: noble, honest, kind, brave, and a few others besides. I made a resolution to be all those things for the rest of my life. It lasted for about a day, I think. I read all the books I could find about her; and the more I read, the more I wanted to be her. I made a serious start in this direction when I was about ten years old. Without ever disclosing my reasons I managed to persuade my mother to let me have my hair cut 'en boule', just like Joan in the picture. Seven years later and it's still cut the same way. It suited me then. It suits me now.

Thinking back, I suppose I have always been a strange sort of girl, never quite happy being who I was, dumpier, more ordinary, than everyone else around me. My face was too round, my hair too thick. At my primary school I was 'a dreamer', or so my teachers often said. 'Bright as a button. Such a pity about her spelling' ran one school report. Dyslexia was diagnosed. I didn't mind that much. It made me different, distinctive, for a while at least. Besides, I reasoned, Joan of Arc couldn't read and she couldn't write either. And she managed well enough, didn't she? I found out about all sorts of other worthy people who had done good and great and exciting things in their lives, who had changed the world – Louis Pasteur, Mother Teresa, Mongolfier, Francis of Assisi. But to me these were mere fleeting interests, no more. Joan of Arc, La Pucelle, Johanne of Domrémy, the Maid of Orléans, always remained my real mentor. And as I grew up she became my abiding soulmate.

Just last year, when I was sixteen, I was told we would be moving house. I didn't want to leave at all. I loved my life in Montpellier, and everything about it. I was happy where I was, with my school, with my friends. But my father, who is a plastic surgeon, had been offered a job elsewhere, a better one, which was far too good an opportunity to turn down, so he said. I protested, of course, but it was no use. The decision had been made. 'And anyway,' said my mother, 'at least Joan on the staircase will find a good home. It'll be the perfect place for her.'

'What do you mean?'

'Orléans,' my father said. 'We're moving to Orléans.'

On my way upstairs that night I spoke to Joan, face to face, and silently. 'You'll be going back where you belong, back to Orléans, Joan, where you lifted the siege and drove the English out, where you rode triumphant through the streets, your standard fluttering over your head. We're going to live there. I'm going to walk where you walked, be where you were. We'll be together.'

There were no more protests from me after that, and indeed all my anxieties about moving very soon vanished. It wasn't the end of anything. On the contrary, it was quite definitely the beginning of something. I felt it in my bones even then.

I wheedled my mother into letting me have the Joan of Arc picture to hang in my new bedroom in Orléans. She wasn't too difficult to persuade – I think she was pleased that I still liked it so much after all these years. My father was, of course, delighted that he wouldn't have to pass Joan of Arc on the stairs any more. He said as much. 'Every time I look at her on my way to bed, she says the same thing: "And have you done enough for France today, Monsieur Hardy?" Gives a man a guilty conscience. As far as I'm concerned you can stick her where you like – just so long as she can't see me and I can't see her.'

So now I had my Joan of Arc all to myself in my new room. I hung her above my bed. Neither my mother nor my father really knew how much she meant to me, because I never told them. I never told anyone. I didn't want her ridiculed – and, I suppose, I didn't want *me* to be ridiculed either. I didn't want her even discussed. They were great ones for discussing everything, my parents. To discuss her would be to share her, and I didn't want that.

Now that Joan was in my room she became even more my secret familiar, my guardian angel and my talisman. I would reach up and touch her face every night before I went to sleep; and in times of trouble I would even talk to her, but quietly in whispers, so no one could ever hear me. It sounds silly, but I began to hope for, even to expect perhaps, replies to my questions, solutions to my troubles. None came, of course. I so much wanted to hear voices, as she had. I listened for them, longed for them, but none came.

As time passed, I talked to her more and more often, for my troubles were many. Worst amongst them was the isolation I felt at my new school. I didn't know anyone, and no one seemed to want to know me – except, that is, for Marie Duval. Whenever she talked to me, Marie Duval made me feel I was the most important person in the world to her. I can't think why she took to me as she did because she always had friends enough and plenty fluttering around her. There was a kind of serenity about her, a serenity I'd known in only one other person, in Joan, in my picture.

One day our black and white cat, Mimi, fifteen years old and all the brothers and sisters I had, just went off and never came back. Day after day I went miaowing round the streets, tapping her saucer with a spoon. I came home one evening to the news that a black and white cat had been run over at the bottom of our street. I wept all night long, brimful with wretchedness. The next morning I was looking up at Joan, for some crumb of comfort, I suppose, when a sudden bright hope flashed through me. Why had I assumed the worst? There must be hundreds of black and white cats in Orléans. Perhaps Mimi was just lost and couldn't find her way home. I should go on looking, but further afield perhaps.

So it was that I found myself that same afternoon after school walking along the river towards my favourite place in Orléans, a place I'd often visited before, the river

bank opposite the site of the Tourelles, the English fort that Joan of Arc had captured hundreds of years before to raise the siege of Orléans. I sat down at the river's edge and watched a flotilla of canoes trying to negotiate the fast water under the bridge. A pair of ducks flew in, landed and swam towards me, bobbing comically. I laughed, and felt suddenly overwhelmed by feelings of complete well-being, of boundless optimism. Mimi would come back when she was good and ready, she'd gone off exploring. I should just stop worrying.

I looked up across the river at where the Tourelles had once stood, shading my eyes against the sun. The place must have seemed impregnable to Joan, to her soldiers, yet time after time they had stormed the walls. Again and again the English had beaten them back, and every time Joan had rallied her soldiers to the attack. She was first up the ladder, first over the ramparts, her standard whipping about her in the wind. All about her now the cheering soldiers poured over the walls. The defenders were forced back and back, and were finally overwhelmed. The slaughter was bloody and terrible. As her soldiers celebrated, I saw Joan turn away from them. I saw her crying up against the wall, out of joy, out of relief, out of horror.

It was strange. Down here by the river, I could see it all in my mind's eye so well, so distinctly. She was short, sturdy and dark – dumpy even, just like me. Yet, in my picture at home she was tall and elegant, with the face of an angel – a slim angel. I decided I preferred the Joan of the Tourelles – the Joan of my dreams.

Day after day I came back to the same place – I confess, not to look for Mimi any more, but simply to dream the same dream. I could never lose myself in it for long though. Some earthly distraction or other would bring me back to now – a lorry rumbling over the bridge, the raucous laughter of the canoeists paddling past, or a bird hopping past my feet, usually a sparrow. There was one sparrow in particular, I noticed, that came back and back. He would stand and watch me first with one eye, then the other. So I took to feeding him, to tempt him in even closer. However much I fed him, he always came back for more. And if any of his friends tried to join in the breadcrumb feast, he'd very soon see them off. I could always tell him from the others – he had a white patch on his throat. He was a scruffy looking ragamuffin of a sparrow, but a real character. I called him Jaquot.

Every time I came now, Jaquot would be waiting for me, and I liked that. I really think he looked forward to our meetings as much as I did. He seemed to learn when to leave me alone so I could dream my dreams in peace. When one day I spoke to him it seemed the most natural thing in the world. I told him all about Joan of Arc, about my picture at home, about how she'd stormed the Tourelles and relieved Orléans. I swear he was listening to every word! But when I'd finished he was simply a greedy sparrow once again. In the end I think I went down to the river as much for Jaquot as for Joan of Arc. As for Mimi, I hadn't forgotten about her. I just knew she'd come back. Somehow I was quite sure of it.

*　　*　　*

The first I heard of it was on a Monday morning. When I got to school the place was buzzing with excitement. Marie Duval came running up to me 'We've been chosen!' she said. It wasn't entirely obvious to me what we'd been chosen for. So I asked her. Each year, it seemed, one school in Orléans was selected, and from that school one seventeen-year-old girl was chosen to be Joan of Arc, chosen to ride through the streets on a white horse dressed in silver armour and carrying her standard. Whoever was chosen would lead the entire procession. It would be in May, May 8th, on the anniversary of the relief of Orléans, just four weeks away. May 8th? May 8th? May 8th would be my seventeenth birthday!

It was some immediate encouragement to me that half the school, being boys, must be disqualified. But there were at least four hundred girls and about a hundred of those, I calculated, would be seventeen or thereabouts. By that afternoon almost every one of those eligible had put herself forward for selection, a hundred and ten in all, including Marie, including me. A hundred and ten to one. Yet I knew as I stood there looking at the great long list of hopefuls, that I would be the one to be chosen. I had no doubt about it. We all had to write an essay – 'The life and death of Joan of Arc'. We had two weeks to finish it and hand it in. The ten best essays would be selected, and for those ten there would be final interviews conducted by the Headmaster and the Mayor of Orléans, and then the winner would be announced.

As I walked home that afternoon I knew for certain that all of this had been meant – the picture of Joan I'd grown up with, the move from Montpellier to Orléans, my new school being chosen for the May 8th celebrations, and the fact that my birthday on the 8th May would make me seventeen and therefore eligible to be the Joan of Arc they were looking for. It wasn't too good to be true. It was going to be true. It was going to happen. I would write the essay of my life: researching diligently, checking every spelling. I would type it out on my mother's wordprocessor, so they didn't have to read my scrawly handwriting. I'd get it done on time, no procrastinations, and submit it. As sure as night follows day, it would be one of the chosen ten. And then, and then. . .

For two weeks I never once went near the river. Jaquot was abandoned. I confess I scarcely ever thought of him. I delved in the library and read as I'd never read before. Then I settled down and started to type, enlisting the spellcheck on the wordprocessor almost constantly. There would be no mistakes. My mother kept saying I mustn't get my hopes up too much, that after all I'd only just arrived at the school, that there were a hundred other girls all beavering away at their essays just as I was. But at the same time she was encouraging me to do my best. She's a writer herself, a journalist, so she knew what she was talking about – in this instance.

'Write it for its own sake, for her sake, Eloise. Try to get under her skin. Try to find the girl behind the legend.' That was good advice. I knew it and I took it, but I didn't tell her I had. I didn't tell her either that I knew I was going to win anyway, that it was all fate, all a meant thing. She'd be sure to scoff at that. My father was scoffing quite enough already for both of them. 'Lot of old flagwaving drumbeating claptrap, if you ask me. All this dressing-up and parading up and down about something that happened hundreds of years ago. Bit of fun, maybe; but you shouldn't go taking it so seriously.'

When it came to it, though, he was the first to read my essay. After he'd finished he took off his glasses and looked up at me. There were tears in his eyes. All he said was, 'Poor girl. Poor, poor girl. How she must have suffered.' My mother said she never knew that I could write that well. I knew, too, that it was far and away the best essay I'd ever written. I was quite sure, as I handed it in, that it would be one of the chosen ten. I hoped Marie Duval's would be another. So, when the Headmaster announced the winners, I was pleased when her name was read out, and wildly excited when I heard my own, but not in the least surprised. Everyone else at school *was* surprised, my teachers in particular; but none of that bothered me. There were a few cruel mutterings about how I must have been helped, but I ignored them as best I could and simply looked forward to the interview and to my inevitable selection as Joan of Arc.

I was nervous before the interview, even though I knew I was going to win. As it turned out, the interview was short and sweet. The Mayor looked just like mayors should look, jovial and well-fed, but worthy with it. He leant forward and asked me from under his twitching eyebrows: 'So, Eloise, why do you want to be Joan of Arc then?'

'I've always wanted to be Joan of Arc,' I replied. 'Ever since I was little.' It was an answer they clearly weren't expecting, and I was pleased about that.

'Can you ride a horse, Eloise?' the Headmaster asked.

'Yes, but not as well as Joan could,' I said. Just be truthful, I kept telling myself. Joan was truthful, always truthful.

There were a few other questions about how long I'd lived in Orléans and where we had lived before, but none of them was searching enough to worry me. The Mayor's endlessly twitchy eyebrows made me smile, so that my laughter came easily – I was so relaxed that I was almost sad when it was all over.

There were only two more to go in after me. Once the last interview was over, we didn't have long to wait. The Mayor and the Headmaster came out together. I could hear my heart pounding in my ears.

'Believe you me, this has been a very difficult choice to make,' began the Headmaster. 'There is no question in our minds who wrote the best essay. It was so good, so outstandingly good, that the Mayor has decided for the first time ever, to publish it as an integral part of the May 8th celebrations. However, we both feel we must take other matters into consideration. Accordingly, on account of her remarkable essay, we have chosen Eloise Hardy – as runner-up. But as you know, Eloise has only been living here in Orléans for a few weeks, a very short time. There can only be one Joan a year, I'm afraid. And our choice for Joan of Arc was born in Orléans and has been living here all her life. She, too, wrote a fine essay, and she interviewed well too. So our Joan for this year is Marie Duval.'

Not me! Not me! Marie had her hands to her face, and there was clapping all around me. The Mayor was kissing her on both cheeks to congratulate her, and I found myself doing the same thing like everyone else. Her cheeks were wet with tears, her tears and mine. 'I'm sorry,' she said. And I knew she meant it.

'Maybe another year,' said my mother when they came up to my room to console me later that evening. 'And, after all, you are having your essay published. That's much more important.'

'You win some, you lose some,' my father added. He kissed the top of my head and tipped my face upwards so that I had to look him in the eye. 'And what do they know anyway?' he said.

They were both kinder, more attentive to me in the days that followed than they had been since I was little. And at school I discovered that Marie Duval was no longer my only friend. Perhaps my essay had earned me some respect; or maybe it was through my losing that I had gained everyone's sympathy. Either way, I basked in it. So it wasn't a complete disaster after all – that was what I kept telling myself anyway. Telling myself was one thing, believing myself another.

The picture above my bed was for me no longer of my Joan of Arc, but of Marie Duval. It was too painful a reminder. I took it down and put it in the back of my cupboard. Out of sight, out of mind, I thought. I wasn't angry at Marie. She had been kindness itself. Not a bit of it. I was angry at Joan. I felt she had misled me, abandoned me; and, talking to the cupboard one night, I told her so.

The river, the only place I could be alone and away from it all, had now become my place of tears. The faithful Jaquot was always there, always waiting for me. Every day now, after school, I would go and sit on the river bank and cry until I had no more tears left to cry. I poured my heart out to Jaquot, and he stayed and listened – providing I kept feeding him.

As May 8th came closer, Marie was ever more fêted at school, and preparations for the great day were becoming increasingly evident not just at school, but throughout the city – bunting everywhere, flags in the streets, and images of Joan of Arc in every shop window. There were reminders around me everywhere I looked. Worst of all was having to smile through it all at school, having to hide my misery. With Jaquot I didn't need to hide anything.

On the night of May 6th I made the decision. I would simply miss school the next day. I would go down to the river and spend all day there with Jaquot. I went off to school at half past seven as usual and made quite sure I was out of sight of the house before I doubled back and made for the river. Jaquot wasn't there, but then I was early, earlier than I'd ever been before. He came soon enough though, hopping up on to the toe of my shoe to ask for his breakfast. I fed him and told him what I'd done and why I'd done it. I had the distinct impression he didn't approve.

'Be like that, then,' I said, and I lay back in the sun and closed my eyes, soaking myself in the warmth of it. For a while I could hear Jaquot pecking busily around my feet. But when I opened my eyes again he was gone, and nowhere to be seen.

That was when I saw the light, a glowing light as bright as the sun, in among the branches of the trees above me. Then it was brighter still, and whiter, enveloping me utterly, until there was nothing to see except the light, and nothing to be heard either. The city had hushed to silence all around me.

The voice came from deep inside the light, deep inside the silence, from far away and close by. 'Talking of sparrows,' it said, 'there was only one creature on this earth who really knew Joan. She called him Belami. He was a sparrow, just an ordinary sparrow like Jaquot; and he stayed with her all her life, almost from the very beginning, and right to the very end. He was her best friend on this earth, maybe her only friend, too. I could tell you more, if you'd like it. I could tell you her whole story, and Belami's too. Would you like that?'

I didn't say yes. I didn't say no. Because I couldn't say a word.

'I'll tell you anyway,' came the voice again, 'because I want to, and because I think you should know all of it, as it was, as it happened.'

I felt myself drifting into the light, into the voice.

❖

CHAPTER TWO

Voices in the Garden

 He was born in the little grey house in Domrémy, the same house Joan had been born in, but fifteen years later – to the day. There was an old nest hole high in the thatch, a safe enough birthplace for a sparrow, you might have thought. This sparrow, though, was still a fledgling, still too young to fly, but did not know it. To him flying must have looked a simple enough business – both his parents did it after all, and with little apparent effort. Lots of birds were doing it, all the time, all around him. He was determined to do it before his brothers and sisters, very determined.

So, one morning, standing on the very edge of his nest hole, and looking out on to a world of white cherry blossoms, the soft sunlight slanting through the green of the beech leaves, he made up his mind to take off and explore this wonderland. He would aim, he thought, for the great spreading apple tree at the bottom of the garden. He fluttered for a few brief seconds on the brink, and felt the lifting power under him for the first time. He let his wings take him and float him out on the air. But at once he was falling. However hard he tried, his beating wings simply would not keep him up. The landing was bumpy and uncomfortable, though not disastrous; but he was still some distance from the apple tree.

He was hopping and flapping his way towards it when he caught sight of the cat stealing through the long grass, slinking low, his tail twitching this way and that. Every bird, however young, knows about cats. The sparrow crouched and was instantly still, still as death. By the time he decided to make his escape, he already knew he had left it too late. For all his wild flapping he could manage little more than a few frantic stumbling hops. At the last moment he cried out, but there was no help, no escape. He was caught, caught and held fast. Death was warm darkness, and mercifully quickly over.

When the hands around him opened, he found himself blinking up into Joan's smiling face. 'Don't worry,' she was saying, 'I won't hurt you. And I won't let Minou hurt you either. I promise. A white sparrow! I didn't know sparrows could be

white.' There was something calming in her voice, and the sparrow lay still in the bowl of her hands, his heart still pumping with forgotten fear. A judiciously aimed stick sent the disappointed cat scampering away back towards the house. 'See?' she laughed, and she settled the sparrow in her lap, talking to him all the while, till she felt the heartbeat stop its racing. 'You've got brown eyes,' she said, 'like me. But I think we've a lot more in common than that. We shall be friends, I know we shall.'

One of his claws became entangled in the thick red wool of her skirt. Joan freed him carefully, gently, and stroked his head with the back of her forefinger. 'They said I would find a friend,' she went on. 'My voices told me so, and they never lie to me, never. Because you are beautiful and because you are my friend, I shall call you Belami. Do you like that? Belami – yes, it suits you. They told me you would come. I needed a friend, Belami, someone I could tell everything to. I wanted to tell Hauviette – she's my best friend – but they said no. They told me to be patient – the blessed St. Margaret is always telling me to be patient – and here you are, just as they promised. They promised me a friend to keep me company, one who would never betray me, and therefore not of humankind, they said. I never understood them, not until now. That's the trouble with my voices, Belami, sometimes they're so difficult to understand. They will speak to me in riddles and I wish they wouldn't. And sometimes, it's so difficult to believe what they say, even when I do understand them. Oh, Belami, the things they say I must do! Of course, I didn't believe in them at all at first. I mean you wouldn't, would you? After all, it's only saints who hear voices, only saints who see visions – or witches. That's what I thought, Belami, that's what everyone thinks. But it's not true. I'm no saint, but I'm no witch either; and I do hear my voices, Belami, I do see my visions.'

She pushed her finger underneath him and felt the tentative grasp of his claws. 'Dear Belami, it's so good to have someone I can tell at last. I think my voices were right. If I'd told Hauviette she'd have thought me mad in the head, or worse. But here I am, talking on and on about myself, when I expect all you want is feeding. Bread and milk, with worms mashed in – how would that be?'

So Joan carried Belami into the house cupped in her hands. She scooted the cat out, and fed Belami for the first time. A few days later and he was flying free. As weeks passed and he grew stronger he was able to fend for himself more and more, but he never strayed far from her and liked to keep her always in his sight. It was on the day of his first exultant flight up towards the sun. He was gliding back to earth when he saw Joan so small, so alone on the ground below. It came to Belami then that he would not be as other birds were, that he would live his life with her, come what may. She had saved him, fed him, and cared for him. Best of all, she needed him. So he would be her friend for life. He would not leave her. He would never leave her.

It was a common enough sight around the village now, Joan with her white sparrow flying above her. Any catapult jokes met with a very frosty response. They were scarcely ever apart. Hauviette said to her once that she never knew she could be jealous of a sparrow, but she was. Wherever Joan went, Belami would follow, and more often than not it was to the spreading apple tree at the bottom of the garden. Here he would sit on her shoulder and listen to her, with half an eye on the aphids and grasshoppers in the long grass below him. When temptation got the better of him he would dart down and help himself; but he would try his best to be attentive because he knew how she loved to talk to him, how she had to unburden herself. He was there for that, there to listen.

Often she'd tell him the same story. It was so miraculous a story that Belami never tired of hearing it. 'To tell you is to remind me it was true,' she told him, 'that it really happened. It helps me to make sense of everything they've told me ever since.' She stroked his wings – she always seemed to do that whenever she wanted him to stay with her and listen. 'It was here, Belami,' she began, 'right here under this tree that I first heard them – over two years ago now. I should have been out guarding the sheep and the cattle with my brothers, Pierre and Jean, and Hauviette and the others, I know that. But, to be honest, any excuse not to be there and I always took it. You watch sheep long enough at their grazing, you watch cows long enough swishing their tails in the sunshine – I'm telling you, Belami, it's enough to bore anyone half to death. Anything to pass the time, and races are best because

I'm good at races. But that day it wasn't even my idea. Down to the river and back, that's what Pierre said – a long way, that is. I think they thought they could beat me over a longer distance. Hauviette hates running, it hurts her legs. So she stayed to mind the sheep and the cattle. Off we went, and I won – by a mile. They weren't at all pleased, as you can imagine. I'm just a fast runner, Belami – you've seen me. I can't help that, can I? And besides it was a race and I've always liked winning better than losing.

'Anyway, the race was over and I was lying there in the sun still trying to catch my breath when Pierre – my own brother! – came up and said that Mother wanted me back at the house. I didn't think, I just went. He made it sound really urgent, the pig. When I got home I found Mother busy at her spinning, and of course she knew nothing about it. You should have heard her. "Why have you left the cattle?" she said. "Do you think they look after themselves? Well, do you?" And she boxed my ears and sent me off back to the fields.'

Belami flew down and perched on her knee. He knew Joan would be crying. She always cried when she got to this part of the story. 'She was so angry with me, Belami, and it was so unfair. I sat down here, right here, and cried my heart out.' She brushed her tears away with the back of her hand. 'I remember there was a sudden rush of wind through the leaves above me, and I remember thinking that was odd, because until then there had been no wind that day, no wind at all. Then there was a silence and strange stillness all around me, as if the whole world had stopped breathing. Over there, just by the well, I saw a white light amongst the trees, and bright like the sun is bright. Then I seemed to be surrounded by it – like being cocooned in a white mist, it was. And out of this mist came a voice calling me – not from inside my head, Belami, I promise you. It was a real voice, a man's voice. He spoke very slowly, as if he wanted me to remember every word he said. I did remember, every word of it.

'"Joan," it said, "Joan of Arc, of Domrémy. You have been chosen by God, by the King of Heaven, to drive the enemy from the soil of France for ever. You will set the rightful Prince of France, the Dauphin, on his throne and see him crowned at Reims. To do this you will have to become a soldier. You will lead the French army into battle, and you will be victorious – that you must never doubt. You will save France, Joan. These things you will accomplish by the grace of God, and in his name. I am the archangel Michael, Joan. After me will come many voices, many visions, all sent by God to help you and to guide you. Listen to them Joan, listen and always obey them. Speak to no man of me, and of your voices, until the time

comes. Meanwhile be good, be strong, have courage. God bless you, Joan, God bless you."

'I saw him, Belami, I saw the archangel Michael. I heard him. He was there, and then he wasn't there. When he had gone and the bright light had gone, I just sat here quite unable to move at first. I was so scared I thought I'd gone mad, Belami. I thought the devil was in me. I got up and I ran. I ran and ran, to the chapel of Notre Dame at Beaumont, my favourite place in all the world, my sanctuary. I always feel safe there. To get there you have to go through Oaky Wood – there's no other way. You know that, Belami, you've been there. There are wolves in that wood and wild boar. And there are supposed to be fairies in there too. I don't believe in all that fairy nonsense, but it's what people say. Anyway, I wasn't frightened of wolves or wild boar or fairies, not that day. It was the devil in me that I was frightened of. I've never run so fast in all my life. Once I reached the chapel I threw myself down on the floor, and I prayed and I prayed and I prayed for the devil to come out of me. My voices answered me almost at once. "Joan, dear Joan," – a woman's voice this time – "Your voices come from God, not from the devil. You must believe that. I am St Catherine and I will speak to you often, I will be with you whenever you need me. So do not fear your voices. There is no devil in you – that is why you have been chosen. Have no fear, have no fear."

'Ever since then, Belami, ever since St Catherine spoke to me that first time in the chapel, I have had no fear of my voices, only of what they ask me to do.' She held out her finger to Belami and he hopped on. She brought him close to her face and looked into his eyes. 'Why me? Why me, Belami? Why would He choose me to do this thing? I'm just Joan, plain Joan. I can sew and spin well enough, though not as well as my mother. I shepherd sheep, I fetch water, I herd cattle. But I am no soldier to go and defeat the English.' There were tears running down her cheeks. 'How can I be expected to save France? I know now that I must, but how? How?'

Belami pecked at her tears, and she laughed at that. She set him back on her knee. 'I ask them how, and they do not tell me. I ask them when, and they do not tell me. "Be patient, Joan," they say, "the time will come." And I do try to be patient, Belami, I do try. But I'm not good at being patient. They should know that, shouldn't they? They should know everything. And meanwhile we hear news that the English and their Burgundian friends triumph everywhere. Their soldiers have only to bark and we French cringe in fear and run off to hide in our castles, our tails between our legs. Every day I am made to wait our enemies become stronger, and we become weaker. I know I shouldn't, but I hate them, Belami, I hate the English.

Why don't they just go home and leave us in peace? I hate the Burgundians even more though. They're of our blood, they're French, and they ally themselves with the English, parcelling up the country, my country, as they see fit. English, Burgundians, they raid and rob wherever they want, and we have no power, nor any will, it seems, to stop them. There's hardly a village left in France that's truly French any more – that's what Father says. Even here in Domrémy there are some who speak openly in support of the Burgundians. And Maxey, our next door village, just down the valley, is all Burgundian. You saw them, Belami, those boys from Maxey who set upon us in the fields only a couple of weeks ago. I longed then to stand and fight, but my brothers sent me and Hauviette off home so we wouldn't get hurt. How many more times do I have to stand by and watch my brothers and my friends come home bloodied and beaten?' She was on fire with rage now. 'And last year when those Burgundian soldiers came – there were only a few of them – did we band together to drive them off? No, we ran. We took our animals and ran for the safety of the Château d'Ile, and the soldiers came and pillaged and burnt the village just as they pleased. And my voices told me then to be patient. They tell me now to be patient.

'I asked Mother once: "Why do we always have to run?" Do you know what she said, Belami? "We do as your father says, as the village council says. It is not for you to question his commands nor their decisions. It's nothing to fret over. The soldiers have been before. They will come again. They are like the storms of winter.

When they are gone, we rebuild, make good. There has been no war in this land for a hundred years. Why should it stop now? Life goes on. We just keep our heads down and keep out of the way – it's all we can do. You think too much, Joan, you always have. Just stick to your spinning and your shepherding and your praying, and with a bit of luck you could make a good wife one day and devout mother. Girls these days," she tutted at me and shook her head, "I don't know."

'So you can see, Belami, even my own mother has long since given up the fight and will not listen to me. I cannot even persuade my own mother. And my voices say that I have to persuade all of France to rise up and drive the English out. But how will I make them believe it can be done, when I do not know myself how it can be done? Oh, Belami, I only wish you could talk. Do you believe I can do what my voices say? Do you? Do you? Oh, talk to me Belami, talk to me.'

As time passed Joan went less often to the fields with the cattle. She might drive them out to graze with the other children, but would always find some excuse to go off. She told Hauviette she needed quiet, that she was going to pray. And it was true, she would spend every hour she could wandering the Oaky Wood alone, or praying in Notre Dame at Beaumont. She was never really alone, of course, for Belami was never far from her side. Sometimes, particularly when she was at her prayers, he would keep his distance, knowing how she liked to be on her own with her voices. He stayed close by though, always hoping for a glimpse of her saints – St Margaret or St Catherine perhaps – but to his great disappointment he never saw nor heard anything of them. He could see she was often deeply troubled and upset by what they told her, so much so that sometimes she couldn't bring herself to speak of it, even to Belami.

She talked to him mostly of her family, and of Hauviette, about how odd they thought she had become recently, how quiet and distant. It was her father that worried about her, more than anyone else, it seemed. 'You know the worst of all this, Belami?' she told him. 'I am deceiving my own father. By not telling him of my voices, of what they say I will one day have to do, I am deceiving him. And he loves me so much, and he trusts me too. We're so alike, him and me. He knows me so well, as I know him. Sometimes, Belami, I find him looking at me very strangely. It's as if he knows something. You know what he said, only yesterday? Out of the blue it was. Father was talking of Robert de Beaudricourt, the Captain of the castle at Vaucouleurs, and what a fine soldier he was. All I said was that given half a chance (and if I wasn't a girl, of course) I'd go off and be a soldier, and I'd drive the English out of France once and for all. He looked at me hard and suddenly became very angry. 'Don't you ever speak of such a thing, Joan,' he says. 'I had a dream once, a dream that comes back and back to haunt me, a dream that you would one day run off with the soldiers.' My brothers sniggered at this. Father banged the table and glared at them. 'It is no joke,' he stormed. 'I tell you, if Joan ever went off with the soldiers I would drown her myself in the river, with my own hands. There could be no greater shame for all of us. Speak to me no more of soldiers, Joan. Be content that you are what God has made you, with what God wants you to be.'

'There are times, Belami, and that was one of them, that I so long to tell him what it is that God really wants me to do. But I cannot. My voices forbid it. To do what I have to do, what God tells me I must do, I must wrong my own father. I must hurt him. Yet he is the one man on this earth I will ever love, my voices have told me as much. How he will hate me, Belami, how they will all hate me.' She wept bitterly at the thought of it.

Belami had taken to waiting for her outside the chapel at Beaumont while she went in to pray. She was always a long time at her prayers; and besides, it was often warmer for him outside, and Belami loved to feel the sun on his feathers. She would often be overwhelmed by tears when she came out, but not this time. Her eyes were bright with excitement. 'The moment has come, Belami. I feel like an arrow released at last from its bow. Just now, in the chapel, Belami, the blessed St Margaret came to me and said that I have to go to Vaucouleurs, as soon as possible. I have to see Robert de Beaudricourt himself. I am to tell him to send me to the Dauphin at Chinon. I am to go to fight the English. It is the beginning, Belami, it is the beginning.'

CHAPTER THREE

❖

For France

It was several weeks before Joan could arrange things. Vaucouleurs was a dozen miles away through the forest. She would need an escort, somewhere to stay, and most important, a reason for going. Otherwise her parents would become suspicious and would never allow her to leave at all. In the end luck lent a helping hand, or fate perhaps. Joan's favourite uncle, Uncle Durand – he was a cousin really, but Joan had always called him Uncle – paid the family a visit. He just happened to say to her that she must come over and stay one day soon, that her Aunt Joan hadn't seen her in a long time.

'She could come now, when I leave,' he said. 'Why not?'

'She's work to do here,' her mother replied, rather tartly.

'We can do without her for a few days,' said Joan's father. 'It'll be good for her to get away for a while. She's not been looking herself lately. Let her go.'

And so it was arranged there and then. When Uncle Durand went the next day, Joan would go with him.

Sitting under her tree with Belami the evening before she left, Joan was beside herself with excitement. 'Can you believe it, Belami?' she said. 'Do you know where Uncle Durand lives? Not two miles from Vaucouleurs! And he knows Robert de Beaudricourt. He knows him! My uncle, he's a kind man, and godly too. He will listen to me. He will believe me, I know he will.'

Belami was there the next morning as Uncle Durand and Joan set off into the mists of the forest. She waited until the village was well behind them before she told him. She first made him promise faithfully he would never tell anyone what she was about to tell him. She didn't tell him everything, only as much as she thought he needed to know. Uncle Durand sat in stunned silence on his horse as she told him, his eyes never leaving her face. 'So you see, Uncle, if you do not take me to Robert de Beaudricourt at Vaucouleurs, where my voices tell me I must go, then he will not send me to the Dauphin at Chinon, and I will not be able to lead his army into battle against the English. I will not be able to drive them out of France, nor to have the Dauphin crowned King of France, King of all the French. Without you, none of this can happen, Uncle.'

Uncle Durand rode on for some time before replying. 'I should take you straight home, Joan, and tell your father. That's what I should do. But I cannot, can I? I promised you I would say nothing and I will keep my promise. But what am I to do, Joan? What am I to make of you? You could be lying to me, making the whole thing up for all I know; or perhaps you are deluded and mad in the head. But if not, then you must be truly blessed. I shall help you, Joan, because I have always known you to be a good and honest and God-fearing girl, and because there's a light in your eyes that makes me want to believe in you, want to help you.

'But there's another reason, too, why I'm going to help you, Joan. I once heard a story, a legend if you like, about a young girl from these parts who would one day drive the English out for good and save France. Maybe the story is a true one, a prophecy, and not a legend at all. Maybe you are the one, Joan. I hope to God you are. I may live to regret it, but I will follow my hope and help you all I can, all I can, dear Joan. But we'll have to tell your aunt, we cannot keep it from her.'

Joan reached out and took his hand in hers. 'I knew you would,' she said. 'Thank you Uncle, thank you.'

But her Aunt Joan was not nearly so easy to persuade. She believed her – that wasn't the problem – she had other serious objections. 'You shouldn't go anywhere near that Robert de Beaudricourt,' she said. 'He's a soldier, and all soldiers are the same – rough, coarse creatures. That castle's no place for a girl your age. I'd never forgive myself.'

'Nothing's going to happen, Aunt,' Joan replied. 'I'll have Uncle with me, and besides I can look after myself.'

'And he drinks too much,' her aunt went on. 'Everyone knows it. He won't listen, Joan. He won't believe you. Your uncle and I, we believe you because we love you, we know you.'

'If you believe me, Aunt,' said Joan, 'then you must believe my voices too. It's my voices that tell me I must go to the Dauphin. Robert de Beaudricourt can get me to the Dauphin. He's the only person who can. I must go, Aunt, can't you see?' Her aunt still looked doubtful. 'I'll be all right. I'll have Belami with me too, as well as Uncle Durand!'

'That sparrow,' tutted Aunt Joan. 'What is it you see in him? He goes everywhere with you. I don't mind outside, but I don't like him in the house – I've told you.'

'He loves it here,' Joan replied. 'You've got no cats, and he loves you too because he knows you'll help me, because you believe in me. So tomorrow, Aunt, when we go to Vaucouleurs, I will go with your blessing, won't I?'

'Of course,' said her aunt, her eyes filling with tears. 'It's just that I fear for you, I fear for what will become of you.'

'But how can you fear for me when I have God on my side?' Joan exclaimed.

They set off early the next morning. Belami flew up and perched himself high on the castle wall as Joan and Uncle Durand rode into the courtyard below. They had to sit there and wait all morning, and all the while Joan had to endure the coarse banter of the soldiers. Several times she had to restrain Uncle Durand from boxing their ears. Then, at long last, two men came striding out of the castle. Both were in armour, swords at their side. 'That's him,' Uncle Durand whispered, 'and that's Bertrand de Poulengy with him.' Uncle Durand, stepped forward. 'My Lord, we sent word we wanted to see you. It's important, important for France.' Robert de Beaudricourt tried to ignore him, but Uncle Durand blocked his path determinedly. 'My lord, I have brought my cousin to see you. She is from Domrémy. What she has to say to you may save us all, may save France.'

'What do you mean? What are you saying?' He was looking down at Joan, towering over her.

'I come to you in my Lord's name, Robert,' Joan said, her eyes looking back into his, unflinching. 'I come to tell you that you must send a message at once to the Dauphin. You must tell him not to engage in any battles with the English until I am there at his side. Tell him that I shall lead his army into battle and give the English such a beating that they will all go running back home where they belong. Once this is done I shall be there to lead him to his coronation in the cathedral at Reims. Tell him, Robert. Do it for me, do it for France, do it for my Lord.'

Robert de Beaudricourt's laughter echoed round the courtyard. But the man beside him was not laughing with him. 'And who,' scoffed Robert de Beaudricourt, 'and who – if I may be so bold as to ask – who is this Lord of yours?'

'The King of Heaven,' said Joan quietly. 'It is he who has sent me to you, Robert, he who has sent me to save France. My voices have told me.' For some moments Robert de Beaudricourt did not seem to know quite what to say.

'Did you hear that, Bertrand? She's another of these mad visionaries. The King of Heaven! Why, you insolent hussy. You could burn for such blasphemy. You dare to claim you speak for God Almighty! And did you hear her, Bertrand? She gives me orders! She calls me by my Christian name, me Robert de Beaudricourt, Captain of

Vaucouleurs! I should throw you to my soldiers for your impudence – they'd know what to do with you all right.'

'That was unworthy of you, Robert, to say such a thing. You should know now that neither threats nor insults will deter me. You speak of daring. I will dare everything, I will dare anything for my Lord in Heaven, for France. Wouldn't you?'

'I could have you whipped, girl,' he bellowed, beside himself with fury now. 'I could have you thrown in the dungeons. How would you like that?'

'I am not frightened of you, Robert. I am frightened of no one. That is how we shall win. I shall show all France that we must not be frightened, that my Lord is with us.'

'Ye gods, Bertrand,' cried Robert de Beaudricourt, slapping his side. 'How she goes on!'

'You blaspheme, Robert. And you should not. When I lead the army, there will be no swearing amongst the soldiers, and no drinking either.'

Robert de Beaudricourt guffawed again, even louder this time. 'Durand Lassois,' he said, shaking his head, 'take this hussy back to her dung heap in Domrémy, and have her father box her ears, before I do it myself.' He turned away. 'She's mad, Bertrand, off her head.'

'Maybe, Robert, but maybe not,' Bertrand de Poulengy replied. Until then, he had not spoken a word, but had been watching Joan with ever increasing interest. 'What is your name, girl? So I shan't forget.'

'I am called Joan, Joan of Arc; and I promise you, you will not forget me.' And to Robert de Beaudricourt, she said: 'I shall be back, and when I come back next time, you will do as I say.' And with that she leapt up on to her horse and clattered out through the castle gate, her Uncle Durand still fumbling with his stirrup and calling after her to wait.

Only Belami was close enough to her to witness her tears of anger and frustration, as she galloped back through the forest towards Uncle Durand's house at Burey. Try as he did, Uncle Durand could not catch her up. By the time she arrived no tears were apparent, but she could not hide her disappointment. When she heard the news, Aunt Joan put her arms around her to comfort her.

'Pay no attention, Joan,' she said. 'I told you, that Robert de Beaudricourt is just a goat of a soldier, and a goat with very little brain, too.'

'I must try again, Aunt, and soon. I cannot fail my voices, I must not. May I come again, Aunt? Will you have me again, after all this?'

'January next,' replied Aunt Joan. 'You shall come again in January. I shall arrange it with your mother. I shall need you then. By then I shall really need you.'

'Need me?'

'Well, if I am right,' she said, looking hard at Uncle Durand, 'and I think I am – in January next year I shall be having my first baby, and I'll need a helping hand.'

Uncle Durand looked completely dumbstruck for a few moments. Then he whacked his horse's rump, gave a great whooping cheer and cavorted around the farmyard like a wild thing, sending the horse and the geese and the ducks and the hens scattering in all directions.

'Your uncle's quite pleased, I think,' said Aunt Joan. 'So you'll come back then?'

'Oh yes,' Joan replied. 'You can count on it. So long as I can bring Belami too.' And they laughed at that and hugged each other tight. Each of them knew that many hardships lay ahead, but in each of them hope was high.

The months that followed were the loneliest Joan had ever known. It wasn't long, of course, before the word was out. Joan of Arc had gone to the great Robert de Beaudricourt and told him how he must send her to the Dauphin, that she was going to save France! She claimed she heard voices. She claimed she saw visions. There were endless strange looks in the village, and mockery, too, from most of her friends. Only Hauviette said she believed her, that she knew Joan would not lie about such things, but that all the same, she should just try to forget all about it and stay at home.

At home it was worse still. Her brothers ostracized her. She had to endure a constant silent rebuke from her mother, and she could see the hurt in her father's eyes every time she looked at him. He wanted her to promise him she would never go back again to Robert de Beaudricourt. For weeks she resisted; but finally, to avoid hurting him any more, she gave in and promised, knowing full well it was a promise she would have to break the next January.

Her only true friend through this dreadful time was Belami. She had no one else to turn to. She would talk to him of the great sadness inside her, of the fears that tormented her, and especially of her voices, how they spoke to her more often now, more urgently. She told him how she already knew that, come January, her life in Domrémy would come to an end, that once she left she would never see it again – her voices had told her so.

'The sooner January comes the better, Belami. Not that I want to leave, but every moment I stay here now is a torture for me. My brothers are ashamed of me. My mother will not even speak to me – she thinks me wilful and stubborn and disobedient – and she's right, I suppose. And my father, my poor father – he just wants things to be as they were before I went to Vaucouleurs. He wants me to be as I was, but he knows in his heart of hearts, in spite of my promise, that I must go there again. He fears for me, Belami, he fears for me. That is why he wants me to stay. I would go now if I could, Belami, I really would.'

January seemed a long time ahead, but that autumn something happened to speed the days on, something unwelcome, but something that was to change how everyone thought of Joan. They had a day's warning. The Burgundians were on the march, and Domrémy was right in their path. Not a small raiding party this time marauding through the countryside, but an army, hundreds of soldiers strong. This time they couldn't just hide away in the safety of the Château d'Ile as they had before – it wasn't strong enough to resist such an army. This time it meant the total evacuation of the countryside for miles around. So Joan and her family were forced to leave the village with all their belongings they could carry, and join the long trail of refugees, and beasts and carts, on the winding road to Neufchâteau. The autumn

rains fell heavily all day. Driving rain it was, that soaked to the skin. The overloaded carts became bogged down in the mud, and many had to be abandoned. Soaked, bedraggled and wretched they arrived in the late evening at Neufchâteau. Here at least they would be safe. Here at least they could find shelter.

The family put up in a dingy house, down a dark and stinking alleyway. They were in a strange place and crowded together in the corner of one room; but somehow happier for it. Now all that mattered was survival. All earlier hurts and bitterness seemed at once forgotten. Belami rejoiced to hear Joan laughing again with her brothers, spinning again at her mother's side.

It was her brothers who sprang to her aid when she needed it most. There was a local lad who had taken a passionate shine to Joan and kept following her about the town like an adoring dog – Belami had seen him long before Joan was ever aware of him. They talked and walked together, and at last he plucked up his courage and told Joan of his love for her. Belami was close by when she tried to put him off. She told him as kindly as she could that she would have no time to marry, that her duty in life lay elsewhere, in the service of her Lord. But he refused to believe her and would not leave her alone, until she told her brothers about him. They were not so kind to him as she had been. He didn't come back any more after that, and when he didn't she half wished he would. Joan could be like that – contrary. 'I so want to be like other girls, Belami,' she told him one evening, 'but I know it cannot be. I did like him, and now I have hurt him too. Why is it that I must hurt everyone I like?'

It was shortly after that the news came through that the city of Orléans was being besieged by the English. It was the worst news they could have heard, for everyone knew that once Orléans fell to the English then there was nothing left to stop them sweeping south and east, enveloping the whole country. 'Cursed English Godoms. They are well named, these English. May God damn them to hell,' said Joan's father. 'Within a year, less maybe, they will have swallowed up all of France. We have to stop them at Orléans. It is now or never.' As he spoke he lifted his eyes and looked straight at Joan, his faith in her unspoken but absolute. At that moment Joan knew that he believed her, and believed in her, and her heart soared. She told Belami about it later: 'If Father believes in me, then I can do it, I know I can.'

They returned two weeks later to find Domrémy in ruins. The church had been burnt to the ground – only the altar was left standing. A few houses had survived the destruction, including Joan's, but that was little enough consolation. Every barn had been either ransacked or burnt. They could rebuild, as they had before; but with their granaries empty, the winter ahead would be long, and hard to endure for both man and beast. Many would not live to see the spring, and they knew it. That first evening back home the family sat around their fire scarcely speaking. Joan's mother stared blankly into the flames. 'How long?' she said. 'How long must we endure this? Why does God not protect us? Do we not pray for it? Do we not beg? What would he have us do?'

'Fight, Mother,' said Joan. 'He would have us fight, and we shall. Believe me, Mother, we shall. It will not be long now, Mother.' Her family looked at her and

every one of them knew then she was speaking the truth.

No one mocked Joan, not any more. When the villagers saw her going off through Oaky Wood towards the chapel of Notre Dame, her white sparrow flying above her head, they knew she was about her work and left her be. There were a few who did not believe her claim, who still ostracized her, who still thought it too fantastical, too impossible. But even those wanted to believe her.

On Christmas morning she was walking with Hauviette to Mass in the ruins of the church. 'I shall not be here next Christmas, Hauviette,' she said, taking her hand.

'I know,' replied Hauviette. 'I shall think of you every day, until you come back.' But Joan knew she would never be coming back, that this was the last time she would walk with Hauviette, her last Christmas at home.

By the time Uncle Durand came for her in the snows of New Year's Day, the family realized these would be their last days all together; but no one had said as much. As for Belami, he buried himself deep in a hole in the thatch up near the chimney, kept himself warm, and waited for the day of Joan's departure.

Uncle Durand stayed only two nights – he wanted to get home to Aunt Joan. There was deep snow the morning they left, and the world was silent about them. It was early. No one in the house was up. She told Uncle Durand she wanted no goodbyes. They would just go. She knew now, though it was still unspoken, that she left with her father's blessing, and her mother's too, and that was all that mattered to her. She wanted no tears, no clinging embraces. Leaving would be hard enough without that.

Belami fed hungrily from the pile of breadcrumbs in her cupped hands. 'You'll need it, Belami,' she whispered. 'We've ten miles ahead of us till we reach Uncle's house. It'll be a cold journey. So eat up.' Belami did not have to be told. He devoured every last crumb before they set off.

Joan tried not to look back at the house. The tears were welling in her eyes, but she knew she must keep them from flowing, just in case she met someone. She did not look back, but she did meet someone. One of her friends, Mengette, was out collecting wood from the log pile outside her house. 'Where are you off to, Joan?' she cried.

'God bless,' was all Joan could reply, and she rode on.

She passed Hauviette's house on the edge of the village, her head down. The last thing she wanted to have to do was to say goodbye to Hauviette, for she knew even then she would never see her childhood friend again. Yet she so longed to see her just once more. She glanced up quickly at Hauviette's window, but she wasn't there. She wasn't sure if she was glad of that or sad.

She crossed herself as she passed by the ruined church. Then they were beyond the village at last and on their way, Belami flying on ahead and darting from tree to tree as they entered the forest – it was the only way to keep warm.

'Are you sure about this, Joan?' Uncle Durand said. It was the first time he had spoken. 'Are you sure you want to go?'

'I do not want to go, Uncle,' she replied, 'but I must. My voices tell me so all the time, and I must obey them. That first time we went to see Robert de Beaudricourt, we were just knocking on his door. This time, with Orléans besieged, he will listen to me, and he will send me to the Dauphin – my voices have promised me. Within a year, Uncle, you will see Orléans liberated, the siege lifted; and you can come to see the Dauphin crowned at Reims. It will happen, Uncle, because I shall make it happen, because my Lord in Heaven wishes me to make it happen. But first, I think, we shall have a baby to care for, won't we? Aunt Joan will be waiting for us. Come on, Uncle, I'll race you!'

And she thundered away through the snow, leaving Uncle Durand looking after her, and shaking his head. 'If anyone can do it, Joan can,' he said. The sparrow had flown back and was hovering over his head. He looked up at him. 'Isn't that right, Belami?' And Uncle Durand spurred his horse on through the snow, muttering as he went 'What the devil am I doing talking to a sparrow! Sparrows can't understand. They can't talk. They can't even sing, not very well anyway.'

Up to that moment, Belami had always liked Uncle Durand – he had been the first to trust Joan and to help her. But now he wasn't so sure that he liked him that much after all.

CHAPTER FOUR

What is it About that Girl?

It was as well they left when they did, for a raging blizzard closed in behind them and cut off the road for days. Just as well, for Aunt Joan too, that they reached her that evening, otherwise she could have found herself marooned in her house and with no help at all. She was already in labour when they arrived, and young Joan was at her side all the way through her pain. She knew what to do – it wasn't the first time she had turned her hand to midwifery.

All through that long night she had no thought of the English, nor of the Dauphin, nor of Orléans. Belami looked on from the flickering shadows grateful for the shelter from the storm outside. The child came bawling into life at last just before dawn, a girl child with dark hair like Joan's. They all huddled together in the warmth of the bed, the precious baby between them. When all the exhilaration, all the marvelling was over, and only fatigue was left, Joan's thoughts turned inevitably to the future, to her mission. Lying beside them, she said: 'I may not be here to see it; but I tell you, well before this child is my age there will be no English Godoms left in France. As soon as the snows clear, Uncle, we must go to Vaucouleurs. This time Robert de Beaudricourt will listen. You see if he won't. I shall make him.'

Yet it was not as straightforward as Joan had hoped or imagined. It took many days before the snows melted and they could set out for Vaucouleurs. Even when they finally got there, Robert de Beaudricourt refused to see her. But she would not be put off. Soon everyone in the castle, in the town knew of the peasant girl in the red skirt from Domrémy. They knew what she had come for, too, and why she waited all day and every day in the castle courtyard. For Joan, and Uncle Durand, and for Belami too, it was a long cold vigil. Belami was frozen, even out of the wind in the nooks of the castle walls. But numb as he was, he knew he had to keep his wits about him. There were hungry, keen-eyed sparrowhawks all around, and Belami was just what they were looking for – a well-fed sparrow, with his mind on other things.

It wasn't until their third visit to the castle that at last someone came out to see them, but it was not Robert de Beaudricourt. It was his friend, Bertrand de Poulengy, who had met Joan the year before, and had never forgotten her.

'It's no use your waiting, Joan,' he told her. 'He won't see you. He thinks you're out of your tiny mind. His words, not mine.'

'And what do you think, Bertrand?' Joan asked.

He looked down at her, and it was a while before he replied. 'As a matter of fact I don't agree with him. Don't ask me why, but I believe you. Besides, as I see it, we've nothing to lose by believing you, except France. And we're fast losing that as it is.'

'Then talk to Robert, tell him.'

'I have, Joan. I've done little else since I first met you. But he's Captain here, and he just won't listen.'

'And I won't go away.'

'I know it,' Bertrand replied. 'I can think of only one possible way out of this. I have a friend, a good friend, a soldier like me, who would stop at nothing to drive the Godoms away – his name is Jean de Metz. If you could first persuade Jean, then Robert would listen to him – I know he would. I have already told him all about you; but he's a down-to-earth sort, sceptical, to say the least. He thinks I've lost my head over you.'

Joan laughed at that. 'So when can I meet this Jean de Metz?'

'Not here. Not now. Robert would be bound to find out and he hates conspiracies. Let me bring him to you, Joan, in town, somewhere quiet where we can talk.'

So it was arranged, and a week later in Vaucouleurs at the house of Henri and Catherine Le Royer, good and trusted friends of Uncle Durand, Joan met Jean de Metz for the first time. She was sitting there spinning with Catherine when he came into the room, a towering bear of a man. He waved everyone at once from the room so that he was left alone with Joan – but they were not quite alone. Unseen, and unmoving in the shadows, Belami sat perched high on top of the cupboard, watching, listening.

'So you're this Joan, are you? You're Bertrand's little friend?' Joan ignored him, and went on with her spinning, not at all daunted. 'Do you know who I am, girl?' he roared.

Joan looked him full in the face and spoke very softly. 'You are Jean de Metz, and you have a very loud voice, but not loud enough, it seems, to frighten the

Godoms out of France. If you want the Godoms out of France, as I do, as God does, then you must do what I say. When you leave this room you must take me to that stubborn dolt, Robert de Beaudricourt, and you must persuade him to send me to the Dauphin. I tell you, Jean, before mid-Lent I have to be on my way to the Dauphin at Chinon. There is no one in the world, Jean, neither King, nor Duke, nor any other who can regain the kingdom of France for the Dauphin. There is no help for this kingdom but me. I should much prefer to stay home where I belong and spin beside my mother in Domrémy. But I must go and do what must be done, since God wishes it. Whether you help me or not, I shall do it. I shall walk to Chinon, and on my own, if I have to.'

Jean de Metz could hardly believe his ears. The brashness of the girl, the insolence! Yet he admired her spirit.

'I wonder,' he said. 'Do you fight as well as you talk, as well as you spin?'

'I could learn,' Joan replied. 'But I shall need a good tutor.'

'When? When must you start for Chinon?'

'Now rather than tomorrow. And tomorrow rather than the day after.'

Jean de Metz sat down in front of her, and took her hands in his. 'Can you really beat the English Godoms?'

'Yes, Jean,' said Joan. 'With God's help and yours, I will go to Orléans and lift the siege.'

'Just like that.'

'Just like that. But I shall need a little help. Will you help me, Jean?'

'Leave your spinning, Joan, and follow me,' said Jean de Metz, and with that he turned on his heel and strode from the room. Joan went after him.

'Where are we going?' she asked.

'First to Robert de Beaudricourt,' he said. 'Then to the Dauphin at Chinon, and then to Orléans. It's what you wanted, isn't it? And I have a feeling, Joan, that sooner or later you always get what you want. Is that right?'

Joan linked her arm in his as he walked. 'Sooner or later,' she laughed. 'And sooner is always better than later.'

Bertrand went with them, Uncle Durand and Henri Le Royer too. But only Joan was allowed with Jean to go inside to see Robert. Belami, like the others, found himself shut out in the courtyard. He perched on the wellhead and fluffed out his feathers against the cold.

'You know what's going on in there, Henri?' said Uncle Durand. 'She's winning her first battle. I understand now how it's done. It's simple really. She just thinks she's going to win and doesn't ever give in. She never gives in. That's the whole secret. You know something else, Henri, I think this may be the most important thing either of us will ever do as long as we live.'

And even as they sat there they could hear Joan's clarion voice ringing out from inside the Great Hall. 'Have priests examine me if you like. Have the Pope himself question me. I should not mind. All I ask is that you send a letter to the Dauphin. Tell him I'm coming. Do it now, Robert, or it will be too late, too late for you, for the Dauphin and for France. In God's name, Robert, stop your shilly-shallying.'

As the argument raged inside – more a monologue than an argument – all of it quite audible, a crowd gathered in the courtyard to listen. 'Will you look at them all!' said Uncle Durand. 'It seems as if the whole world and his wife want to know what's going on in there, and how important it is too.'

'You hear what they're calling her?' said Henri Le Royer. "The Maid". Already they are speaking of her as the saviour of France. For goodness' sake, she's just seventeen, and a farm girl.'

'She's a lot more than that,' said Uncle Durand. 'That's the whole point, Henri. I know it. They know it. And soon all of France will know it.'

At that moment the doors of the Great Hall opened and Joan came bounding down the steps two at a time. She flung herself into her uncle's arms. 'He's going to do it, Uncle! Robert is sending a letter to the Dauphin. As soon as he replies, I shall be going to the Dauphin at Chinon.' Then she whispered in his ear: 'It will all be as my voices said it would be, just as they promised me. Didn't I tell you? Didn't I tell you?'

As they rode away out of the castle through the clamouring crowds, a bewildered Robert de Beaudricourt stood on the steps watching her go, Jean and Bertrand on either side of him. 'Why?' he said. 'Why on earth did I agree to do it? I didn't mean to. When they get this letter in Chinon, I'll be a laughing stock, a laughing stock. What is it about that girl?'

'There is God in her, Robert,' said Jean de Metz. 'That's why I did what I did, why you did what you did, and why the Dauphin will do just as she tells him to.' He clapped Robert on the shoulder. 'Don't worry about it, Robert. She'll make your name in history. Yours too, Bertrand, and mine. God help the poor English Godoms, when she gets amongst them.'

'God won't help the English,' laughed Bertrand. 'I think you'll find Joan will make quite sure of that!'

But still Joan did not leave at once for Chinon, as she had hoped. Robert de

Beaudricourt was having second thoughts. He sent a succession of learned priests to question her and examine her, to be quite sure she was who she claimed she was. All of them came suspecting her to be a witch, and left overwhelmed and convinced by her piety, by her sincerity. As word of the miraculous Maid got about she found herself invited into the houses of the great and the good – many of them, until now, known sympathizers of the English cause. Much encouraged, Joan always went and was always disappointed. These people, she soon discovered, were not in the slightest bit interested in joining her to drive out the English as she had hoped, but wanted instead only to have their ailments healed by her, by her 'miraculous' powers. After weeks of this nonsense and still no reply from the Dauphin, Joan had had enough. She stormed into the great hall of the castle, and sought out Robert de Beaudricourt, her eyes on fire with anger.

'You told me I could go! You told me! Do you want me to sit here while France collapses all around us? This very morning at my prayers, my voices told me news of the Dauphin's army, how they have been driven from the field at Rouvray. I told you that he should not let his soldiers take the field, not until I was with him. Did you not tell him? Does he want to lose all of France to the English? Does he want to lose his kingdom?'

'I have heard nothing of any battle at Rouvray, nor anywhere else,' said Robert de Beaudricourt. 'If there had been a battle, do you not think I should have heard of it?'

It was two days later when the news came that the Dauphin's army had indeed been routed, and at Rouvray just as Joan had said. At long last his doubts were over. Robert de Beaudricourt believed her. Even he could see that there was no other way she could possibly have known of the battle. It had to have been some kind of divine revelation. She did not need to wait any longer. She could go to the Dauphin, he said, but even now he would not part with a penny piece to help her on her way. In the end it was the people of Vaucouleurs who raised the sixteen francs needed to buy Joan the horse she would need for the journey.

Dozens wanted to go with her. But dozens would be conspicuous. In the end there were just seven of them: Jean de Metz, Bertrand de Poulengy, their servants, Richard the Archer, a deaf-mute fabled for his strength and his uncanny accuracy with a bow and arrow, and Joan herself. Enough to afford some protection, they hoped, but not too many to attract attention. Their road would take them through the heartland of occupied Burgundian territory. Even if they did manage to avoid the marauding Burgundians, the forests were thick with robbers and malcontents.

It would be a journey fraught with danger.

Joan could not have cared less about all this. She just wanted to be on her way. 'They worry so much, Belami,' she told him one night. He always perched close to her at night, close enough so she could reach out and touch him. These days, it was the only time Joan could be alone with him. With Joan so lauded and fêted wherever she went, they could scarcely ever be alone as they used to be, and they both missed the quiet intimacy of each other's company. 'We'll get through somehow,' she went on. 'I know we will. My voices say we will. They want me to dress as a man. They tell me that as I am a soldier now, I must look like one. But I so like my red skirt. I know it's wilful, but I've always loved it, and I'm keeping it, whatever my voices say. I've obeyed them in everything else, haven't I? '

But in the end she did not keep it, not as a skirt anyway. It was not her voices who persuaded her though, not directly anyway. It was Jean and Bertrand and Uncle Durand. They were all quite adamant. 'Either you go disguised as one of us, as a soldier,' said Jean,'or you don't go at all. For God's sake, Joan, the whole country is talking of no one else. Do you want to end up in some ditch with your throat cut before you get to Orléans? Well, do you?'

For once Joan had no answer. 'Madame Le Royer has agreed to do the work,' Jean went on. 'I've got a pair of my servant's breeches that'll fit. Your Uncle Durand will lend you his tunic, and Bertrand's young cousin has a pair of boots your size. I have arranged it all.'

'No you haven't,' said Joan. 'It is my voices that have arranged it, as they arrange everything in the end. I had thought to defy them in this, but I see I cannot.' They were mystified at this, as they were by so much of what she said. 'Very well,' she went on, 'but I shall still wear my skirt. It shall serve as a man's cloak. I shall make it myself. My voices shall have their way. And you can have your way, Jean, only if I can have mine. Remember that and we shall always work well together.'

Bertrand smiled. 'That's our Joan – victory out of defeat. We win the argument, but she wins the war.'

There was an afternoon and evening of cutting and sewing before Joan's suit of boy's clothes was ready: a grey tunic over black breeches and boots, a scarlet cloak over her shoulders. She paraded for them round the room.

'You will do,' said Jean de Metz. 'You are a soldier now, Joan. You may have no beard, but you're one of us.'

'Then I am content,' Joan replied. 'For I would be as my soldiers, eat what they eat, sleep where they sleep. But I am a soldier still without a sword.'

Strangely it was Robert de Beaudricourt who provided the sword. When they left the next day all of Vaucouleurs was there to see them off. 'Go carefully, Joan,' said Robert de Beaudricourt, suddenly fonder of her than he ever thought possible, and with that he unbuckled his own sword, and handed it to her. 'Go, and do what must be done.'

'You have been an obstinate old coot, Robert,' said Joan, mounting up. 'But you have given me a start. God bless you for that, and for this sword, too. The rest is up to me now, and God.' And blowing a farewell kiss to the Le Royers, to her uncle and aunt and the babe in arms, she rode away towards Chinon, never once looking back.

They did not stop to rest once that first night, wanting to distance themselves as quickly as possible from Vaucouleurs. As it turned out no one followed them nor were they attacked. It was rather the rain that was to prove their worst enemy on the three-hundred-mile journey. Through Burgundian territory they travelled by night whenever they could. It was hazardous going, and not just because of the enemy, who were everywhere about them and bound to be looking for them. But every river they came to was in flood. To Joan, even rivers were no barrier. To her every precious hour wasted on a detour meant another dead Frenchman. She would ride up and down the bank surveying the river for the best crossing place. Then she would plunge her horse in. The others soon learnt that her judgment always proved safe, that every swollen river was fordable if they followed her, if they crossed exactly where she did.

Belami flew above them, beating his path through the torrential rain. It was no weather for sparrows either, but Belami did not mind. Now she was on her way, Joan was happier than he had ever seen her. And if Joan was happy, then so was he, no matter what the weather.

There were friendly houses, and abbeys, like the one in St. Urbain, where they could rest in safety and dry out. Joan slept where the others slept, the only girl amongst six men; but none of them thought of her as a girl any more, not even Bertrand, who was usually a great one for the ladies. Joan insisted they travelled by day now, for there was no time to waste. Movement at night along the muddy roads was often slow and on several occasions they had got themselves hopelessly lost in the darkness. But there were risks in travelling by day, and they knew it.

They had left Gien, and for once the sun was warm on their backs. They were in French territory now, and safer or so they thought. They were riding through the forest when they suddenly found their way blocked by a dozen unsavoury-looking ruffians, their swords drawn and glinting, their arrows readied and aimed. From down out of the trees all around came several more of them, flitting like shadows. Within seconds they found they were surrounded. The leader of the ruffian gang stepped forward.

'And which of you is the Maid of Domrémy?' he demanded.

'Him,' Joan was laughing and pointing at Jean de Metz. 'But he has a beard, so I suppose you might not believe me. It's me, you dunderhead. I am the Maid. You want to kill me, do you, or rob me? Well, you can if you like. We can't stop you. But all I have on me are these two rings.' She wriggled her fingers in the air. 'See? Oh, and my sparrow up there on that branch. You could eat him, and you could sell the rings, and you could kill me. But what would it profit you? The sparrow is tiny and probably tasteless. The rings are worthless and I'll be just another body in a ditch. Or is it a ransom you're after perhaps? Ah, I see from your eyes that I have hit the mark. Well, you're wasting your time there too. First, the Dauphin has no money, by all accounts. And second, if he had he'd not part with a penny of it for me, that's for sure. So you see you'd be wasting your time.' The robbers stood there speechless as she went on. 'Shall I tell you something? On this ring it says 'Jhesus Maria'. I was sent here by Him, by our Lord in Heaven, to drive out the Godoms for ever. With His help, and with yours, I will save France. Well, what will it be? A couple of worthless rings, or the freedom of France? Take your pick.'

The robbers backed away from her, crossing themselves, and let Joan and her companions pass on their way. All of them, except Joan, expected an arrow in the back, but none came.

As they neared Chinon they came to the shrine of St Catherine at Fierbois. Here Joan was happy to stop for an entire day, not just to rest the horses, but to say Mass. 'I have not said Mass in a week, Belami,' she said, as she unsaddled her horse outside the chapel. 'Going to Mass is like drinking water to me,' she went on. 'I would die inside without it.' All day she prayed at the chapel, guarded by Richard the Archer and Jean and Bertrand, all on edge now after their brush with the robbers in the forest. When she had finished praying, she at once dictated a letter to be carried on ahead to the Dauphin. 'Write that he will be alone no longer, that I shall soon be there to come to his aid, that I know from my voices many things that will be to his own good and the good of France, that I must therefore see him as soon as I arrive, that there is no time to waste.'

❖

CHAPTER FIVE

We Need a Miracle

 By the time she rode into Chinon the next day the whole town knew of her coming and was out in the streets to greet her. They crossed themselves as she passed, and many of the sick reached out to touch her stirrup and seek her healing blessing. She was bewildered at all this adulation; but her heart soared when she saw the hope and faith in their eyes.

To her astonishment and dismay though, when she came up to the castle gates she was told the Dauphin would not see her. For two whole days she paced her lodgings in a fury of frustration. With Jean and Bertrand counselling patience, she received the Dauphin's endless messengers as courteously as she could – patience had never come easily to Joan at the best of times. She sent back the same message every time: 'Say to the Dauphin that I have come a long way to see him, that the King of Heaven has sent me to raise the siege of Orléans and afterwards to lead the Dauphin to his coronation at Reims. I shall say no more than this, however many messengers he may send me, until we meet in person.'

Both Jean and Bertrand were sent for and questioned about this strange visionary from the farmyard, this unlikely saviour of France, but in spite of all they said on her behalf the Dauphin still would not see her. On their third morning in Chinon, Joan was sitting disconsolate on her bed, and Belami was on the window ledge singing his heart out for her, to cheer her flagging spirits, when the Dauphin's messenger arrived yet again. This time, at long last, it was to summon her to the castle. So with Jean and Bertrand at her side, and Richard the Archer going ahead, she walked, almost ran, the short distance up the hill and over the drawbridge.

As she was crossing the courtyard a man rode up to her and laughed haughtily at her from high on his horse. 'So you're the famous Maid,' he scoffed, looking her up and down. 'By God, one night with you and I could teach you a thing or two.' Jean went for his sword at once, but Joan put a hand on his arm to restrain him.

'You shouldn't say such things,' she said quietly, 'nor use God's name as you do, particularly as you are so close to your own death.' The rider guffawed, put his spurs to his horse and rode off towards the drawbridge. Joan watched him go. He was halfway across the bridge when his horse stumbled and fell catapulting him into the moat. From all over the castle courtyard they ran to help. Joan crossed herself. 'Poor man. They cannot save him, nor his immortal soul either,' she said sorrowfully. She turned away and looked up at the castle walls. 'Well Dauphin,' she went on, 'here I come.'

Belami flew off and circled the castle looking for the best and safest vantage point. There were pigeons perched everywhere, but in the end he did manage to find a space on a crowded ledge. He was there just in time to see Joan come striding into the Great Hall, Bertrand and Jean behind her.

It was a vast and magnificent room, under a high vaulted ceiling. There were flaming torches all around the walls – fifty, a hundred of them maybe – and underneath them a milling crowd of courtiers, of bishops, of noblemen and their ladies, all bedecked and glittering in their finery. At one end of the room was a throne on a dais where the Dauphin sat waiting for her. Joan walked the length of the hall, the crowd parting for her to let her through. A hush fell about the hall. For a moment or two Joan stood before the throne, looking the Dauphin full in the face.

'Do you not bow to your Dauphin, girl?' he said.

'Yes,' Joan replied coolly. 'I would, but you are not he. You are not the Dauphin. You are trying to trick me, to test me as I knew you would, as my voices warned me you would. They tell me everything, you see. You can deceive me, but you cannot deceive God. Since you seem to insist on playing silly games, I shall find the good Dauphin for myself.' She sprang up on to the dais, and surveyed the great throng of people in the hall. 'Ah,' she said, 'I see him.' She jumped down and plunged into the crowd.

It looked for a moment to Belami as if she was bobbing a curtsy to a stone pillar. There was a sudden gasp of astonishment. 'Kind Dauphin,' – she seemed to be talking to the pillar – 'I am Joan, known as the Maid. The King of Heaven sends me to you with the message that you shall be anointed and crowned king in the city of Reims, that you will be the lieutenant of the King of Heaven, who is also the King of France.' From behind the pillar came only a face at first, a sheepish face, flaccid, with bulging frightened eyes.

'It's not me who is the Dauphin, Joan,' he said, and he pointed back towards the throne. 'There, there is the Dauphin.'

'In God's name, noble Prince,' said Joan, stamping her foot, 'it is you who is the Dauphin, and none other. We have no time for such games. The English will be at your gates in weeks, and you play games. Would you have me stop them, or no?' She came closer to him. 'I must speak with you, alone and now.'

She took him by the arm and led him away into a side chamber. They made a strangely incongruous pair, the nervous knock-kneed potbellied Prince of France with weasly wandering eyes, and the sturdy country girl dressed up as a boy soldier. She was talking earnestly to him as they went, talking as if she had known him all her life.

Belami tried every window in the castle but still could not find them. In the end he returned to his ledge, drove off the noisy pigeons and waited. Down in the hall they waited too. It was some time before the two of them emerged. When they did the Dauphin looked a different man. The pallor had left his face. His eyes had stopped their wanderings. He even stood straighter, and he was holding her by the hand as if she was a long lost sister. The hall was silent at once.

'Let it be known throughout my k-kingdom,' – he spoke with a stutter, but as he went on the words came with increasing confidence, 'that this Maid, this Joan of Arc of Domrémy, is a true messenger of God. She has the eye of God. She knows my prayers, things I have not divulged even to my confessor.' There were some barely suppressed sniggerings at this. '*And, and*, she has it on God's authority that despite what many of you think – and I know you think it – God knows that I am no bastard, but the true and rightful son of my father, and therefore the true King of France.' He turned to the Archbishop of Reims who was standing close by. 'Archbishop, Joan would have you anoint me and crown me King in your cathedral, where all French kings should be crowned.'

'But it is impossible,' the Archbishop replied. 'There are twenty thousand English between here and Reims, and they still besiege Orléans. Besides, why should we believe this chit of a peasant girl?'

'The English will not be there for long, my lord Archbishop,' said Joan. 'My voices tell me I will drive them out, and my voices come from God. Don't you believe in God, my lord Archbishop? You should, I think.'

To hear this country girl lecturing the Archbishop was too much for some, and there were angry mutterings around the hall. Just then, a young man, resplendent in gold and blue, stepped forward. He was clearly a man to be respected for everyone fell silent at once. 'If the Dauphin believes her, then I believe her too,' he declared, and he declared it loud enough for everyone to hear. He bowed to Joan.

'I am the Duc d'Alençon, Joan, just recently come out of an English prison, my ransom paid. I know of you from my good friends, Jean de Metz and Bertrand de Poulengy, and neither of them is inclined to wishful thinking. If you say you are sent by God, then I believe you. I for one will join you and fight by your side for as long as it takes.' He knelt before Joan, took her hand in his and kissed it.

'You are very welcome,' Joan replied. 'The more such men are gathered in God's name the sooner we shall win.' The Dauphin clapped at that, and then everyone was clapping with him and cheering, such cheering as the castle had never known in all its history.

Up on his ledge, Belami's heart swelled with pride. When he flew off it was to soar high above the castle towers singing out his joy like a lark – as nearly like a lark as he could manage anyway.

Joan dined at the castle that evening with the Dauphin, and two of the great dukes of France, the Duc d'Alençon and the Duc de la Trémoille. They talked only of how they could raise the siege of Orléans, of how long it would take to gather the army. But Joan saw even that first evening how weak the Dauphin was in his resolve, one moment fired with determination, the next his head shaking with doubt and despondency. One moment he was the cat that had got the cream, the next he was wondering if it had gone sour.

'But what if we fail, Joan?' he whined. 'Even if I throw my whole army against these walls of Orléans, I could still lose, couldn't I? Lose my army and I lose France. We need a miracle.'

Joan tried to soothe away his fears. 'Why else do you think I am here, gentle Dauphin? But the miracle will not happen unless we make it happen. The walls of Orléans will not just fall down. I cannot blow them down with trumpets as Joshua did. We must knock them down and the English with them. Give me command over your army and with God's help I will do the rest.'

All evening, aided and abetted by the Duc d'Alençon, she coaxed and badgered and cajoled and inspired the Dauphin, until finally he had to give way. 'The army is yours, Joan,' he said at last.

Later they all went out together on to the darkening watermeadows, below the castle.

'I don't suppose you've ever ridden a horse, Joan?' asked the Duc de la Trémoille.

Joan snorted at that. 'Just give me a horse, my lord duke, and you will see whether I can ride.'

Thinking she would never manage him, the Duc de la Trémoille brought her a great war horse, a giant of a charger. Joan did not hesitate. Without ever setting a foot in the stirrup, she leapt up, gathered the reins and galloped off. Afterwards the Duc d'Alençon led her into the castle courtyard and gave her a lance. To his amazement, and everyone else's, she tilted like a veteran. When she had done, Belami flew down to perch on the end of her lance.

'You tilt like a soldier,' said the Duc d'Alençon, running up to her, breathless with admiration.

'That's because I am a soldier,' Joan replied, 'God's soldier, and I shall be to the day I die.'

'But maybe,' said the Duc d'Alençon, 'you should not dress like a soldier, Joan. I mean, some people will not like it, you know. Women should dress like women.'

'My fair duke,' Joan laughed down at him. 'You talk to me of clothes! You dress up like a peacock, yet you are a man, not a bird. I want only to look like a soldier. I dress as I do because my voices say I must, because I must live my life amongst my soldiers, live as they live, be as they are. And know one thing about me, my fair duke, I care not one fig what people like or do not like about me. I care only to obey my voices. I have asked them often about this and they tell me I was right to put away my women's clothes, and they tell me, too, that I must never again dress as a woman – nor as a peacock, come to that.'

The Duc d'Alençon knew when he was beaten and gave up. 'Do as you will then,' he said, 'but for pity's sake, Joan, you cannot go around in those ragged old clothes, looking like someone's servant. If you are to lead us, Joan, then you must look the part.'

'Very well,' Joan replied, 'but understand, whatever I wear, my scarlet cloak never leaves me. It will take me through my battles, so that when I am wounded – and I shall be – no one will know it.'

'Ah Joan,' said the Duc d'Alençon. 'I shall be at your side to protect you. I would never let that happen.'

Of all the people at court, it was only the Duc d'Alençon she liked to be with. To some she was either a curiosity or a saint, and they treated her accordingly. To others, and these were many, she was some kind of a witch, casting her wicked spells over the Dauphin. Many of the army marshals were already jealous of her sudden power and influence, and resentful of her youthful vigour. Some of the nobles and their ladies, polite on the surface, were stung by her popularity with the people. She read hate in their eyes, and there was envy too. Of all of them she trusted only the Duc d'Alençon, 'my fair duke' as she always called him.

She had just a few days of tranquillity and peace with the Duc d'Alençon and his Duchess at their castle nearby in the countryside, and she knew even then it would be the last such days she would ever know. Here the Duchess had made for her some new clothes, not just suitable for any soldier, but as she said, 'for a great soldier of France'. They presented her with the finest horse they had, 'to chase the Godoms out of France'; and the three rode, and sang, and walked and talked together for hours on end. Parting from the Duchess, when it came, was hard. 'Look after him for me, Joan,' she said, embracing her. 'He's such a hot-head.'

'Fear nothing,' Joan replied, 'I will send him back to you as safe and well as he is now, or even better.'

Back at the Dauphin's court at Chinon she found herself treated now like a royal princess. She had her own rooms high in the Coudray Tower inside the castle itself. This suited Belami fine. He found he could fly in and out just as he pleased. She had her own chapel too and her own priest to go with it. She could hear Mass everyday. She lacked for nothing – she even had servants now, and a page.

Her page was called Louis, a slip of a lad, barely fourteen, just three years younger than she was. When they first met he was tongue-tied with awe, for by now Joan was even more famous than the Dauphin himself.

'Well, Louis, what does a page do? I've never had one before,' Joan asked him.

'Look after you, I suppose,' said Louis.

'But I can look after myself,' replied Joan. 'I always have done.'

'What must I do then?' he asked her.

'Be a friend to me, Louis, that's all I ask. And be a friend to my Belami. Feed him when I forget. And, Louis, if ever I get too big for my boots – and I fear I shall – then prod me and remind me I am just Joan from Domrémy, and must always remain so. Will you do that for me? Will you promise?'

After that, young Louis went everywhere with her, half an eye on Belami and half an eye on his young mistress – prodding her vanity whenever it appeared. He did this often and gently, particularly when she became overwhelmingly imperious or presumptuous which she was inclined to be from time to time. Joan came to trust in him absolutely, and so did Belami. He would sit on Louis' finger, on his shoulder, on his head, anywhere – providing he got fed, of course.

Joan longed to be gone with the army to Orléans; but, like Robert de Beaudricourt before him, the Dauphin began to lose his nerve after his first flush of enthusiasm. His marshals complained bitterly at the prospect of having a peasant girl leading their army. Only the great Marshall La Hire was firm in his support. 'We have not done so well without God's help,' he said. 'If she is from God – and she may be – then let's have God on our side. We need him.' The bishops too sowed new doubts about her in his mind, and the doubts preyed on him. He sent countless bishops and learned clerics up to her tower to interview her; and he sent ladies to examine her purity, to make quite sure which she was, girl or boy. The Dauphin himself accompanied her to Poitiers where she had to endure long days of interrogation before more bishops and more learned clerics. Joan bore it all stoically, though on occasion her patience wore very thin. They would ask her such silly questions, and she was always inclined to give as good as she got.

'Do you believe in God?' one asked her.

'Yes,' she snapped back, 'and better than you.'

'Can you give us some proof that you are sent by God as you say you are?'

'By God's name,' she replied. 'I have not come to Poitiers to perform miracles. Lead me to Orléans, and I will show you the miracle for which I am sent.'

In the end it was not her answers that convinced the Dauphin, but the crowds that clamoured after her wherever she went. Just to ride alongside her through the people dispelled any lingering doubts he might have had. He could see for himself how fervent was their faith in her, how she had renewed their spirits and their hope. She was hailed everywhere as the God-sent saviour of France. So, at long last, and to Joan's great joy, he gave the word that she was to have all she needed, that no more obstacles should be put in her way, that the army should be made ready to march on Orléans.

More new joys awaited her, and unexpected ones, too. Knowing how sad it made her to be away from her family, how she missed them, the Duc d'Alençon had sent for her brothers, Pierre and Jean, without telling her. They arrived one day at Chinon and the Duc d'Alençon led them at once to her tower. When all the tears and hugging were over, Pierre noticed Belami perched by the fire warming himself.

'You haven't still got that infernal bird, have you?' he said.

'Yes,' said Joan, 'and my skirt too.' And she threw her cloak about her shoulders. 'See? They're all I have left of home – but now, God be thanked, I have you as well. And Father, Mother – are they angry with me for leaving you all so suddenly and without asking, without even saying goodbye?'

'No Joan, not any more,' said Jean. 'They are proud of you, so proud, as we are.'

Wherever she went now her brothers rode with her, along with the Duc d'Alençon, Jean de Metz, Bertrand, and Richard the Archer as her bodyguard. She also had two heralds who went ahead of her, and, of course, young Louis who never let her out of his sight.

The Duc d'Alençon arranged for the best armourer in Tours to make her a suit of armour. She wanted it plain, she insisted, with no arms emblazoned. And so it was done. He had a lance made for her, too, and a battleaxe. The armourer wanted to make her a sword as well, but she refused.

'My old sword from Vaucouleurs I shall give to my page, Louis. He has often asked for it so that he can protect me,' she told him. 'My new sword, the sword I shall take into battle was forged in heaven.' The armourer may have been amazed at this, but such was his faith in her, he did not for one moment doubt her. 'So you need not make me a sword. But you can fetch it for me, if you will. Go to Fierbois, to the chapel of the blessed St Catherine. Tell the priests – they will know me for I was there not long ago – tell them to dig down into the ground behind the altar. There they will find a sword. It will be engraved with five crosses. It may well be a little bit rusty, but the rust will come away easily enough.'

So he went, and sure enough, just as she had predicted, that was exactly where the priests found it. When the armourer had cleaned it up, he brought it back to her at Chinon with two scabbards, one of crimson velvet – a present from the people of Tours – and another in a cloth of gold that he had made himself.

'Too fancy. Both of them are too fancy,' she said to Louis when the armourer had gone. 'I shall have a leather one made like all the other soldiers.'

The ladies at Chinon made her a standard to her own design: white for purity, with fleur de lys, and two angels embroidered on it, and 'Jhesus Maria' in large letters, for this was her motto, her battle cry. It was now the battle cry throughout the French army as they set out at long last on the march to Orléans, with Joan at their head and Belami riding high and happy on the point of her standard.

Joan slept every night in her chain armour, to get used to it. She ate with her soldiers and prayed with her soldiers too. Priests went ahead of them singing *Non Nobis* and the *Te Deum*. She let it be known that because her army was fighting in the name of God there would be no swearing, no looting, no womanizing. She would have none of it. Even amongst all the great nobles and dukes, and marshals – including Marshal La Hire himself who was not known for his gentility– she would not tolerate bad language and most certainly no blasphemy. She was fierce in this and would brook no argument about it from them nor from anyone else. Indeed, as they were all soon to discover, this seemingly sweet natured, simple country girl, once roused, could be fearsome in her anger.

It very soon became clear to Joan that some of the marshals of the army were treating her as little more than a sort of mascot, a lucky talisman. They murmured amongst themselves about the indignity of having to accept Joan as an equal. To them she was merely an illiterate, ignorant peasant girl, unfit to be a soldier, and untried in any campaign. It was more than many of them could stomach. She might be useful for raising the morale of the soldiers, they felt, but that was all. So they told her nothing of their plans, and did not consult her on strategy, but instead humoured her gently, conforming to her wishes that there should be no crude soldier talk, no pillaging, and in particular no women. Grudgingly they accepted all she had decreed. Joan was the only woman in the five-thousand-strong French army that marched from Blois towards Orléans, along the south bank of the Loire river that rainsoaked April. With them went thousands of cattle and sheep and pigs and wagonloads of provisions, all for the relief of the besieged people of Orléans.

❖

CHAPTER SIX

Go Godoms,
in God's Name, Go!

There was a rainbow over Orléans when she first saw it. The roofs of the city shone across the river under the distant sunshine. But as she stood there on the river bank, she was not completely happy. She sent for La Hire and the other marshals at once. 'There is the river between us and the English,' she said, quite unable to hide her anger and her disappointment. 'Tell me, how are we to fight the English if we are here and they are there? Why did you not tell me how things were?' La Hire tried to explain that it was safer to approach from the south, that the English were stronger to the north of the city, that they would wait for the Governor of Orléans, the Bastard of Orléans as he was called, to come across with his boats, then the army could cross. It would be safer that way, he said.

'Safe!' she blazed. 'In God's name, are we here for our safety? I am no one's poodle, La Hire. I am the envoy not just of the Dauphin, but of God. Remember that. Never forget it.' And she stormed off leaving him lost for words. All he could do was marvel at her. 'When he comes,' he whispered under his breath, 'my friend the Bastard of Orléans is in for a hell of a surprise, I think.' Fully fifty paces away by now Joan whirled around pointing her sword at him. 'Yes, indeed he is. And you mind your language, La Hire!'

That afternoon the Bastard of Orléans came across the river to greet Joan. Her reputation, her fame, had gone before her. Like everyone else in Orléans he had been longing to meet this miraculous peasant girl who seemed to be rallying an entire nation, who had come to lift the siege of his city. But it was not quite the meeting he had been expecting.

'I suppose,' said Joan eyeing him darkly. 'I suppose you must be the one they call the Bastard of Orléans. You're the one who hatched up with La Hire and the marshals this silly notion of coming south along the river to avoid a fight with the English. Are you frightened of them too?'

No one in his entire life had ever dared accuse the Bastard of Orléans of cowardice, until now. He should have been furious with indignation, but instead found himself being conciliatory.

'We thought it wisest, Joan, not to be caught out in the open by the English, with all the beasts and the baggage. We thought it more important to first supply the city – the people are in dire need of what you bring. Then we can march the army in afterwards. After that we can sally out to fight the English whenever we like.'

Joan could see the sense in it and calmed at once. 'Well you thought wrong not to tell me,' she told them all. 'That's all. Remember that I bring you the finest help that ever was brought to a city, since it is the help of the King of Heaven himself. We shall cross now right away. I am eager to see it, to see the people.'

But the marshals looked at one another in some consternation. 'What is it?' said Joan. 'What now?'

'That was just what we had in mind, Joan,' said the Bastard, 'but there is a problem. The wind. We need a fair wind to bring the boats upstream, and I'm afraid the wind is entirely in the wrong quarter. We need it to change. It could be some days.'

'Days! You should know,' said Joan quietly, 'that I don't much like to wait, not when I am about God's work.'

With that she walked away from them down to the river where she fell on her knees and prayed. Belami flew off to be with her. He was fluttering over her, trying to decide where best to land, when the wind gusted suddenly and changed direction, buffeting him out over the river. Joan opened her eyes, breathed the wind in deep, crossed herself and stood up. She turned round. La Hire, the Bastard of Orléans, the Duc d'Alençon, her brothers, were on their knees. Indeed, the entire army was on its knees, wondering at the miracle they had just witnessed. 'Well,' she said, 'you have your wind. So, no more excuses. I want to eat my supper in Orléans tonight.'

Belami settled on her shoulder. 'Ah Belami,' she said. 'If only we could all fly like you. Then we'd have no need of boats or wind, would we? That would be something, wouldn't it?' She laughed out loud as she read the thoughts in their heads. 'No, no my friends, I cannot sprout wings. Come on, off your knees. There'll be time enough for praying in Orléans.'

So the boats sailed across the Loire that afternoon and Joan was ferried across, along with all the beasts and the provisions, and the French army. By nightfall they were at the gates of the city.

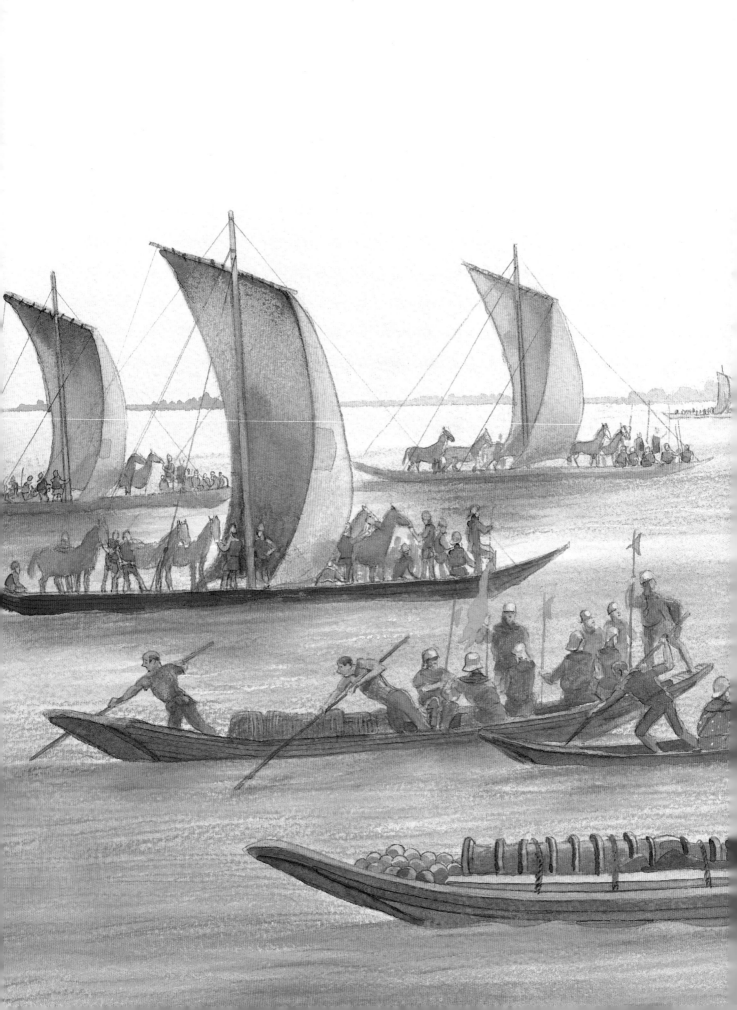

From their forts the English looked on, too few, too surprised to do much about it, except hurl a few obscenities, and fire off a few cannons. But Joan and the French were well out of range of both. Belami was in Orléans before Joan. He could not resist flying on ahead. Below him he could see the streets packed with people, the entire city lit by their torches. After a while he flew back to be with Joan, to perch in pride of place on the point of her standard as she rode in through the city gates and was at once enveloped by adoring crowds. But Belami very nearly came to grief. A torch touched a nearby banner and it burst instantly into flames, singeing Belami's tail feathers. Joan was too busy putting out the flames to notice his discomfort. He did try to tell her, but in all the clamour he could not make himself heard. Once in her lodgings, she seemed to have little time for him. Instead he went and complained to Louis who fed him and stroked him. 'She has not forgotten you, Belami,' said Louis. 'She has a great work to do, and she must be about it. You understand that, don't you, Belami?' Belami understood it perfectly, but he did not like it, not with his feathers all singed.

The room was full of people. La Hire was there at her table as she ate her supper – some bread dunked in red wine, her favourite. So was Jean de Metz and Bertrand de Poulengy, the Duc d'Alençon, her two brothers and the Bastard of Orléans. It was the Bastard and La Hire who were doing most of the talking, arguing between them as to whether or not they should go to Blois for reinforcements before attacking the English. 'Go for your reinforcements, if you like. But not yet,' said Joan. 'I want no blood spilt until I have given the English a chance to retire from their forts.'

'But Joan,' said the Duc d'Alençon, 'we have already sent a letter to the English. And what did you have back but insults? I tell you, they will not leave unless we make them leave. I know these English. They won't go just because you ask them to. For God's sake, let's be at them.'

'My fair duke,' said Joan, 'your wife was right, you are a hot-head. But I tell you, I will spill no blood, English or French, unless I have to. My Lord in heaven says I must do what has to be done, so far as I can, without bloodshed. So, my lord, I shall write another letter. Take this down and have it sent.' She thought for a moment and then began to dictate. 'Talbot, Glasdale, and all you English dukes and soldiers. You see I have come to Orléans as I said I would. I urge you now, before it is too late, to give up the siege and go home to England where you belong. If you do not I shall be forced to attack you in your forts and drive you out. Go, Godoms, in God's name, go.'

The next morning one of Joan's heralds was dispatched to the English under a flag of truce. All day she waited, and still the herald did not return. Joan, becoming more agitated by the minute, paced her room alone. Only Belami was with her. 'Why do they not reply, Belami?' she said. 'Don't they know I mean what I say? Do they think I am frightened? Do they know me so well? For I am frightened, Belami, but not of fighting, nor of dying either, nor of being wounded. I know that one day soon I shall be wounded – here above my left breast, I know it. My voices have told me so. But it's none of these things that frighten me. My voices tell me I must be a soldier, that I must lead my soldiers and fight alongside them. Until now I had not thought of it, Belami. If we fight, then there will come a time when I face my first Englishman sword in hand and I shall have to kill him. I don't know if I can do it, Belami, not look him in the eyes and drive my sword into his flesh. That is what frightens me. Please God they will surrender their forts and just march away. Please God. Where *is* my herald? Where is he?' But by evening the herald still had not returned, so she determined to deliver her message herself.

D'Alençon tried to stop her, so did her brothers. She would listen to no-one. She would have one last try, she said, and forbad any of them to come with her. Alone she strode out over the bridge towards the Tourelles, the strongest of the ring of English forts that surrounded the town. 'You English,' she called out. 'I call upon you in God's name to give yourselves up and save your lives.' But the rest of her appeal was drowned out by a chorus of jeering and whistling.

'Cow girl!' they cried. 'Whore! Witch! Go back to your pigs. We'll burn you to a crisp. Roast whore!'

Joan was not so much angry with them, as hurt, hurt to the quick that they had spoken to her as they did. 'I have done all I can and they will not listen,' she said to the Duc d'Alençon and La Hire, as they walked together sadly up through the town, the crowds thronging about her everywhere. 'Very well, La Hire,' she said. 'Send to Blois for reinforcements. Make your new plans. They want war. They shall have war.'

But even then, as they waited for the reinforcements to arrive, Joan did not give up her attempts at peaceful persuasion. The English lobbed cannon-balls into the city, and still she tried. Every day for three days she went to the walls of the Tourelles and asked the English in the name of God to go. They refused even to send back her herald, but kept him prisoner. On the fourth morning the lookouts saw in the distance the flags and lances of the army from Blois. Joan took five hundred men and led them out under the noses of the English to escort the army

in. Belami flew out over the fort over the heads of the Englishmen who could only look on awestruck as the soldiers from Blois streamed in through the city gates, drums beating, pennants flying. There was no more jeering amongst them, and only a silence, the silence of fear. Belami flew back to Joan. 'Maybe, Belami,' she said. 'Maybe once they see all this, once they see how many we are, how strong, how high our spirits are, maybe now they will leave.'

But they did not. On the contrary, news soon came that Sir John Fastolf was on his way with hundreds of English. On hearing that, Joan was furious. 'Well then, on their own heads be it. Let them come.'

Joan was exhausted. She went upstairs to lie down in her room for an hour or two. Sleep came only slowly. There was such a hubbub in the streets below. The city streets were crammed with soldiers, and her house was always besieged by adoring wellwishers. There was little peace. She did drift away into sleep, but only for a few short moments.

She woke with a jolt and sat up. 'They are fighting, Belami. I know they are. There's blood being spilt, French blood. Someone has ordered an attack. And they have not woken me. Don't they know they cannot do it without me?' She armed herself quickly. She was already mounted in the street, when she discovered she had left her standard behind in her room. She sent Louis back up for it, and he handed it down to her out of the window. Then, with her brothers, Duc d'Alençon and Richard the Archer with her, she clattered through the city, sparks flying from the horses' hooves. She knew exactly where the battle was, where she would be needed.

It was just as well she arrived at the Bastille St. Loup when she did. Repulsed twice, already the French were gathering once again to attack the fort, but they had lost heart. They could see the English high and impregnable on their ramparts, their cannons firing, their arrows raining down on the French. So heavy was the fire that the French could only huddle under their shields. Then they saw Joan riding forward through their ranks, her standard fluttering above her head. It was the spur they needed. With a mighty cheer of 'Jhesus Maria' they rushed the walls, threw their ladders up against them, and then were everywhere upon the English

with such a sudden and unexpected ferocity that within an hour of her coming the fort was overwhelmed.

It did not matter that there were ten other forts around the city still in English hands. What mattered was that after months and months of siege the first of them had been taken. Joan ordered that all prisoners should be spared, the wounded of both sides cared for, and that there should be no looting.

That night in Orléans the bells rang out for a great victory. Joy was everywhere, everywhere that is except in Joan's room. She lay on her bed and wept, wept for the dead, English and French alike, and went to confession. She had not killed. She had not even drawn her sword for fear she might, but she knew well enough she had caused over a hundred English to be killed.

Much against the wishes of La Hire and the marshals, Joan forbad all fighting the next day for it was a holy day, Ascension Day. She went to Mass and then sent her last message to the English. She commanded Richard the Archer to fire it into the English camp. Belami followed him to the city walls, and then the arrow to where it fell. So he was there when it was brought to Talbot, the English commander.

'It is from the cow girl,' he said, and then read it out loud. 'Listen to this. "You, men of England, you Godoms, who have no right to be here in this Kingdom of France, the King of Heaven commands you through me, Joan, to abandon your forts and go back where you belong. If you fail to retreat, I will do with all of you what I did to the English in the Bastille du Loup. I am writing to you for the last time." And she signs herself "Jhesus Maria, Joan the Maid".' He screwed the letter up, hurled it to the ground and stamped it into the mud. 'Who does she think she is?' he cried. 'And who does she think we are to run away? I'll see her burn first!'

Later that evening Joan had her answer. A figure appeared on the ramparts of the Tourelles for the whole city to see. It was unmistakably an effigy of Joan, and there was a notice hung around her neck: 'The Whore of Domrémy!' And then, to whooping cheers from the fort, they set fire to it, and pushed it out over the ramparts.

As Joan watched, the tears welled into her eyes. 'Yesterday,' she said, 'we took one of their forts. Tomorrow we shall take two more, the Bastille de St. Jean de Blanc and the Bastille des Augustins. We shall cross the river and come round behind them.' She knew this was not the strategy the marshals had in mind, but she overruled them. 'I may know nothing of military matters,' she said, 'but remember, I have the hand of God to guide me.'

Such statements made her few friends amongst the marshals and dukes. But she had firm allies and admirers now – the faithful Duc d'Alençon of course, and La Hire and the Bastard of Orléans himself. 'Hasn't she always been proved right so far?' La Hire argued. 'Isn't she winning for us? Isn't she winning for France?' Her critics had no answer to that.

Next morning they attacked across the river, just as Joan had commanded, the soldiers crossing over a hastily built pontoon bridge, in effect a bridge of small boats, and then marching unopposed along the far side of the river towards the Bastille of St. Jean de Blanc. The English garrison saw them coming. They saw how many there were, and how strong too. They quickly abandoned the fort and fell back behind the much stronger walls of the Bastille des Augustins which they knew they could defend more easily. It was some time before Joan, La Hire and the Duc d'Alençon could bring their horses across the river, for the horses were too heavy for the pontoon and had to be ferried over by boat. By the time she arrived, the French army was milling about in wild celebrations at having captured a deserted fort. Joan could see at once that there was little enough to celebrate. And she was right.

Suddenly the English were pouring out of the Bastille des Augustins and charging through the fields towards them. Joan, La Hire and d'Alençon did not hesitate. With a cry of 'Jhesus Maria' on their lips, they couched their lances and rode straight at the English. The rabble of the French army was suddenly no longer a rabble. They were regrouping. Then they were charging *en masse*, coming on at the English crying, 'Jhesus Maria!' A few brave English stayed to fight, and the

battle that followed was swift and bloody; but the rest had taken to their heels and fled to the safety of the Tourelles, the great fortress on the bridge. Joan was content to let them go. 'We want no more slaughter,' she said. 'Besides, two forts is enough for one day. We have done well. We shall leave the Tourelles for tomorrow. It will still be there.'

Joan had been hurt: her horse had stumbled and fallen on her. As the Duc d'Alençon gave her a ride on his shoulders back to the pontoon bridge, Louis going ahead of her with her standard, the whole army cheered till their throats were raw with it. Above her flew a single white sparrow who cheered in his own way, soaring high over the river, then over the city where the great bells pealed thunderously and where every citizen crowded every street and every window for a glimpse of their beloved Joan, their Maid of Orléans, their saviour and already their saint.

Belami was there waiting for her in her room when she came in. She threw herself down on the bed and cried, unable to banish from her head the terrible sights she had witnessed during the battle. Everyone was clamouring to see her, but she told Louis she would see only her dear brothers and the Duc d'Alençon. They all tried to comfort her, but she was quite inconsolable. When they left her that night, she asked Louis to rub her foot for her. 'This pain you can relieve,' she said. 'It is a little thing. Tomorrow, Louis, I shall have an arrow here below my shoulder, but that again will be little enough to bear. Tomorrow by this time, there will be hundreds of French and English dead in the Tourelles. If only the Godoms would just go, Louis, then none of it would have to happen. But what must happen, will happen – my voices have told me so – although I do not understand why. I will never understand why.'

All Orléans knew what Joan and her marshals knew, that once the Tourelles was taken, Orléans would be safe at last. But the Tourelles was not like the other forts. It was quite impregnable. On the south side it was protected by a deep ditch, and on the city side by a great gap in the bridge from the city, a gap far too wide for a man to leap.

Lying in bed that night Joan stroked Belami and spoke her thoughts. 'It will have to be a frontal assault across the ditch, Belami, there is no other way,' she said. 'But those walls are so high and they will be waiting for us. I cannot see how it can be done. I cannot. I cannot.'

She could not sleep, and after a while she did not even try. She prayed constantly and aloud, asking St Catherine, asking St Margaret, asking the Archangel Michael how it was to be done, but none of them would speak to her.

'Why have they deserted me, Belami?' she cried. 'In my hour of greatest need, why have they deserted me? I need to know what to do. Until now our victories have been easy, but not tomorrow. If we try to cross that ditch, we shall be beaten back, I know it. The bloodshed will be terrible. Yet we can do nothing else. So many will die, Belami, so many. I cannot bear it.' That night Joan of Arc cried herself to sleep.

But when she woke the next morning, she woke fresh and ready for battle. 'Come, Belami,' she said, as she left her room. 'Let's get it done.' Downstairs Louis had prepared her a breakfast of a fine sea trout. 'In God's name, no, Louis' she laughed. 'Maybe I'll have it when we return this evening. I'll share it with a Godom for supper, if any live to eat it, as God knows I hope they will.'

The battle for the Tourelles was every bit as brutal as Joan had feared. Time and again the French charged across the ditch to the walls, threw up their ladders and hurled themselves at the English. But each time the English were ready for them, with their arrows, their long lances, their battleaxes and their maces. The very few French who did manage to gain a foothold on the ramparts were butchered at once, their throats cut and their bodies hurled back down into the ditch below. And all the while there was the dreadful roar of the cannon, and the stifling smoke and the screaming and the terrible stench of blood. Yet still they came at the walls, and they came because Joan was always with them rallying them, leading them, her red cloak flying about her, her standard held high, so that all could see it.

The arrow that struck Joan pierced her armour above her left breast, just as her voices had told her it would. The force of it spun her round and sent her tumbling into the ditch. A great cheer went up from the English. Louis was there first, then her brothers and Jean and Bertrand, all of whom had never been far from her side throughout the battle. They carried her from the field. Word soon spread that the Maid was down. The soldiers looked about them for the flash of her scarlet cloak, for the white and blue and gold of her standard. But they could not see Joan, nor any sign of her. They fell back, disheartened; and from the walls above the English cheered wildly, revelling in their triumph.

Hidden from their sight in a nearby wood, Joan lay deathly white on the grass. 'Back to the walls,' she cried and she grasped Louis by the hand. 'Take my standard, Louis. Be me for a while. I won't be long.'

Once Louis had gone she took the arrow and jerked it out. As the blood flowed out on to the grass, the Duc d'Alençon and her brothers did what they could to staunch it. They poured on olive oil. They rubbed it with lard. She hadn't the strength to sit up, but she would not stay lying down. 'I must see what is happening,' she said. 'I must know.' And her brothers helped her to a tree where she could lean and watch. She wept openly now at what she saw. The ditch was full of French dead, but still the ladders were going up against the walls, still they tried. She could see her fluttering standard through the smoke, and Louis waving the soldiers on towards the walls. But she could see too that the soldiers were tired, that it was hopeless to go on as they were. 'Call them back, La Hire,' she said. 'They need food. They need water, they need rest, and I need to pray. When I have finished praying, I promise you I shall find a way to take the Tourelles.'

Stronger now, she mounted her horse again and rode away into a vineyard to be on her own. Here she dismounted and knelt and prayed. Belami, perched on a nearby vine, could see her swaying on her knees, and clutching on to a vine to steady herself. She was a long time praying, but at last she crossed herself and pulled herself up on to her feet. 'My voices have spoken to me at last, Belami,' she whispered. 'We wait out of sight until evening, until the English think we have given up and gone home. Then we attack, and we attack on both sides. The English think the gap on the bridge side cannot be crossed. Until now, we have thought the same. Well, it can. With God's help, it can.'

Joan rode back and summoned La Hire and the marshals, and told them of her plan. 'Have the men march away wearily so the English can see them. Once out of sight, have them hide almost until darkness. Have them pray too. And then, when they attack, have them fall on the English like ravenous wolves.'

Later that evening, with the French army lying hidden in the vineyard and woods, Belami flew over the ditch of death into the Tourelles. The walls were almost devoid of defences now. The English were down in the courtyard celebrating their great victory, and the killing – as they thought – of the Maid. The ale and the wine flowed fast and freely. Through the darkening shadows the French rose up and crept towards the walls, not a whisper, not a sound. Suddenly the English heard the war cry go up: 'Jhesus Maria! Jhesus Maria!' They rushed to the battlements to see the French storming up their ladders, to see Joan already on the ramparts, her standard waving about her. The French poured over the walls into the Tourelles driving the English before them. The English fought fiercely, but the French were all around them now. The gap between the bridge and the fort had been spanned, great planks of wood thrown across the divide until there was enough of a bridge to enable the French to break in behind them. The English looked about frantically, but there was no way out. In desperation, they tried to

escape over the drawbridge, but it was already in flames, the French having sent a fireboat underneath to set fire to it. Those caught in the flames, and that included Glasdale, the English commander of the Tourelles, died a dreadful death. The slaughter everywhere was terrible. Joan could not bear to look upon it, nor hear it. She turned her face to the wall and cried up against it, her hands over her ears.

It was dark by the time Joan led her exhausted, exultant soldiers back across the bridge into Orléans, leaving the Tourelles behind her in flames.

Belami sat now on the pommel of Joan's saddle, to be as close to her as he could, in her hour of triumph. She rode through the torchlit city streets, the rapturous crowds all about her, some cheering, some chanting the *Te Deum* as she passed them by. They pressed so hard upon her, everyone longing to see her, longing to touch her. But Joan longed only for the silence of her room. Once there, once her wound was dressed, she said a fond goodnight to her brothers and her friends, and to Louis, telling them all she needed to be quiet, to be alone. She sat over her supper; not the sea trout – she had that sent to an English prisoner as her gift to him – but her usual supper of bread and wine. She fed Belami some crumbs which, as usual, he accepted eagerly and gratefully. 'It has been a long day, Belami. The longest of my life. Still, we did it, didn't we? With God's help, we did it.'

❖

CHAPTER SEVEN

Joan the Miraculous, Joan the Invincible

 Joan was shaken awake early the next morning, and found Louis bending over her.

'The English!' he said. 'The Godoms!'

'Do they not know when they are beaten?' cried Joan, wincing with pain as she pulled on her chain armour.

Belami flew on ahead of her as she rode through the city streets. Beyond the walls he could see now the two armies drawn up facing each other behind their stakes. The French marshals spurred on by the victory at the Tourelles were about to unleash their army when Joan rode up and berated them soundly. 'What do you think you're about? Do you not know it is Sunday, God's holy day? We shall defend ourselves only if they attack us; but we will not attack on a Sunday. Do you hear me? Give the Godoms the chance to retire with honour, and I tell you they will go. Maybe they will go all the way back to England.' The marshals knew better than to argue with Joan in this mood, so that when she ordered an altar to be made and Mass to be said all the way along the line, none of them dared to object. The French army knelt, their backs to the enemy; and when they had finished their prayers they stood up and turned once again to face the English only to see the entire army drifting away.

'Joan,' said La Hire, his hand on his sword, 'let's be after them. For God's sake, we will not have another chance like this.'

'No,' Joan replied. 'It is for God's sake that we let them go. You will get them another time.'

And so they did, time after time after time. Castles and towns under English occupation for a hundred years and more fell like dominoes before Joan and her army. With the Duc d'Alençon, La Hire and the Bastard of Orléans as marshals of the army she harried the English everywhere, chasing them out of their strongholds. Where they stood and fought, they died in their hundreds, in their thousands, or were taken prisoner. Where they ran, the word spread with them that Joan the Maid, Joan the miraculous, Joan the invincible, was on her way. English hearts quaked, hearts of oak, that until now had never known fear, never known defeat.

Jargeau fell, then Meung, then Beaugency. She was tireless in her conquests, and suffered no one who tried to obstruct or delay her. Louis often had to remind her these days who she was, for he could see, as her brothers did, as the Duc d'Alençon did, that her new found power, the constant adoration of her soldiers, of the people, and her own fierce belief in her cause could sometimes make her impatient, even imperious. She would listen to them all, and for a while she would rein herself in; but always she forgot herself again and Louis had to remind her once more that what she was doing was for God, and in his name, that she was merely his instrument, and nothing more.

'Louis is right. They are all of them right,' she once confessed to Belami, alone in her room in Orléans. 'I do forget myself. But what they do not know is that my time is short. My voices have told me so. How short I do not know, though I have asked them often to tell me. I have still many thousands of English to sweep out of France. I have still to see my king crowned at Reims. If I am impatient, then it is because I must be.' Belami looked her in the eye, and she knew he understood. 'These are the good times, Belami, the victorious times,' she said, stroking his wings. 'But they will not last for ever, and when they are over it will be you and me, Belami, just you and me.'

But the good times were not yet over. Word came that a five-thousand-strong English army was marching south, with Talbot, their great general, in command. Joan and her army went out to find them, but in such thickly wooded country their task was not so easy. The English were marching through the forest near Patay in search of the French. In spite of their scouts each army was blind to the proximity of the other. 'Make sure,' said Joan to d'Alençon, as they rode through the trees in the morning mist, 'that you all have good spurs when the Godoms see us.'

'You think, then, we're going to turn and run when we meet them?' the Duc d'Alençon replied, more than a little hurt at the suggestion.

'Of course not, my fair duke,' said Joan, smiling. 'I tell you, it will be the English who will turn their backs. By this very afternoon they will be defeated and you will need spurs to pursue them.'

At about noon, the French scouts accidentally put up a stag who bounded out of cover. The English saw it and gave chase, with great hue and cry, and so betrayed their position. The French were up on them and amongst them before they knew it.

Jargeau

Meung

Beaugency

In the vicious mêlée of the battle, the glades of Patay rang with the screams of the dying, the hideous neighing of terrified horses, the clash of steel on steel. Within an hour or so it was all over. Four thousand slaughtered English lay bleeding in the mud, and the rest were prisoners, including the great Talbot himself. Here was sweet revenge for the defeat at Agincourt all those years before.

But in the din and confusion of battle Joan had been lost and was nowhere to be found. They scoured the forest calling for her. It was Louis who came across her first. At first he thought she had been wounded, for she was lying up against a tree trunk, and there was blood on her face and on her hands too. When he came closer though, he saw she was cradling the head of an English soldier in her lap. 'He is dead, Louis,' she whispered as he crouched down beside her. 'He died, and without confessing his sins too.' She looked down into the soldier's face. 'There's a boy in my village who looks just like him. Can all this be necessary, Louis? Can God really have meant this?' And when she wept, she wept like a child. That was how the Duc d'Alençon and La Hire found her some time later, her head on her page's shoulder, and wracked with sobbing.

She looked up at them and brushed away her tears. 'I did not want this, and I will have no more of it. I shall go now to Reims and see the Dauphin crowned. Perhaps now the English will have learnt. Perhaps now they will go home and leave us in peace. Then I can go back home to my mother and father, back to my village where I belong.' They helped her to her feet. 'See there is no looting, that all the Englishmen are buried with honour, and the wounded cared for,' she said. 'Dead or living, French or English, we are all God's people.'

There were those marshals, La Hire amongst them, who argued that with the English so weakened, so demoralized, they should at once attack Paris and then drive the English out of Normandy once and for all. But Joan would not hear of it. 'We go to Reims,' she said. 'Let us have our Dauphin crowned the rightful King of France, as my voices said he must be. Paris can wait.'

It was one thing to want the Dauphin to be crowned, but quite another to achieve it. He was grateful to Joan for her victories on his behalf, and heaped upon her great favours and honours. At court she wanted for nothing. He made a solemn declaration that no one living in her village of Domrémy would ever again have to pay taxes, but he would not go yet to Reims. He liked his creature comforts. He was happy enough where he was. Some who had his ear – his scheming adviser, La Trémoille, for one – thought it too risky a venture and told him so. To get to Reims an army would still have to pass through enemy country. 'Why don't you rest a while, Joan?' the Dauphin told her. 'You've done so much.'

In the privacy of her rooms, Joan fumed with frustration. 'I should not say it, but sometimes I feel like kicking him, Belami. I really do.' As it turned out, she did not need to go to that extreme. Other voices – the Duc d'Alençon's for one, and La Hire's too – joined the clamour that at last persuaded the Dauphin he must leave the safety of his castle and have himself crowned at Reims.

The road to Reims was a triumphal one. Town after town opened their gates, handed over the keys to the Dauphin and welcomed their beloved Maid of France, strewing the path before her with flowers. There were a few towns that shut their gates against them. The army did not stop to subjugate them – Joan would not let them. They simply passed around them. She would allow nothing to impede their progress to Reims and the king's coronation.

At Chalons-sur-Marne she found herself surrounded by dozens of children all pointing and laughing at Belami, she thought, who was perched, as he so often was, high on her standard. She looked up. 'See, Belami, see how many admirers you have,' she cried. And then she noticed that Belami, too, was looking skywards. Above him fluttered a cloud of white butterflies that floated down about them now like blown cherry blossom. Belami eyed them greedily. 'Don't you dare, Belami!' Joan cried. 'I'll never speak to you again.'

While the children laughed at this and marvelled too, their mothers and fathers knelt and crossed themselves. Here was evidence, if any were needed, again of their Joan's miraculous powers. Had she not changed the direction of the wind at Orléans? Was she not driving the English out of France almost single-handed? She was a blessed messenger of God, sent by Him. She was their Maid, their saviour. For them the white butterflies were simply further proof of it.

'Well, Joan,' came a voice from the crowd, a voice she knew well. 'I see you've still got your Belami.' It was a moment or two before she found the face that went with the voice – Durand Lassois from Vaucouleurs.

'Uncle Durand!' she cried, and leapt from her horse. She hugged him to her, her heart bursting with joy. He rode with her and her brothers all the way to Reims through the wide open country of Champagne, and all the way they talked of home, of Joan's mother and father, of Aunt Joan and the baby, of Robert de Beaudricourt, of Domrémy. And the butterflies followed them all the way. The temptation became too much for Belami. Luckily Joan was too busy talking to notice his feeding forays amongst the butterflies. Belami was a very happy sparrow, and a very well-fed one too, by the time he first saw the great towers of Reims cathedral.

The people of Reims flocked out into the sunlit streets to greet their Maid, and their Dauphin, and their victorious army. The bells and the cheering rang out over the roofs of the city, and warmed Joan to the heart. 'I think, Uncle Durand, I shall never be any happier again in all my life than I am now.'

She was wrong. She was at her supper that evening, alone in her room with Belami, when Louis came in. 'I know you do not want to be disturbed, Joan, but there is a man outside who claims he is your father,' he said. 'Shall I send him away?'

'Well,' said a shadow in the doorway. 'Are you so grand now that you would send me away?' The shadow stepped into the light and became her father. The two of them clung to each other, neither wanting ever to let go. 'So,' said her father, at last opening his eyes, 'so the sparrow came with you.'

'He'll always be with me,' said Joan. And the two sat down at the table to talk. 'And mother? Is she with you? Is she here?'

'You think a farm runs itself?'

'Is she well? And Hauviette? Have you seen Uncle Durand? He's here too. And anyway, how did you know where to find me?' There were so many questions they talked together all night and were still talking when Belami woke at dawn.

'But after today your work will be done, Joan,' her father was saying, reaching forward across the table to grasp her hands. 'Today, when the Dauphin is crowned, you will have done enough, done all anyone could ever have expected of you. Come home with me, Joan. Come home.'

'You think I do not want to, Father? You think I haven't seen enough of this killing? You think I'm not tired of it. Oh Father, I long to lie again under my apple tree and dream my dreams, to sit spinning beside Mother, to go wandering in the fields with Hauviette. I long for it. But my work is not finished. My voices tell me I may not rest until the last of the enemy is driven from the soil of France. I must listen to them, you know I must. Have they not always been right? Have they not always protected me? They will never abandon me. They have promised me. Dear Father, no more pleadings, no more entreaties; else you will weaken my resolve. And no matter what happens, I must be strong for France, strong for my Lord in Heaven.'

On the day of the coronation they breakfasted together with Uncle Durand and her two brothers and d'Alençon. It should have been a joyous affair, but it was not. The impending parting of their ways hung over them like a shadow.

As she rode at her king's side that day through the streets to the cathedral, she was blind to the rapture and adoration all around her, deaf to the blessings they called out to her. Belami sat on the pommel of her saddle and she stroked him with her finger, just as she did when she was in bed and crying herself to sleep.

All through the glittering ceremony, the anointing of the royal head, and the crowning itself, the tears welled in her eyes and would not be held back. Tears of joy, the people thought, but they were not. This crowning was all she had strived for. She had achieved the impossible in just a few short months, yet she could not rejoice in it.

That same evening her father prepared to leave for Domrémy. 'I came here to bring three children home,' he told her. 'I leave with none. Neither of your brothers will leave your side. No father in France can be sadder than I am today, and none prouder either. Go then, if you must, and chase the Godoms out of France. But when you have done it, come home Joan. We shall be waiting for you.'

Joan could not bear to watch him go, but ran inside and hid herself in her room. 'Sometimes, Belami,' she said, sitting on her bed, hugging her knees and rocking back and forth, 'sometimes I know things even my voices have not told me. I shall not see him again, Belami, nor hear his voice, not on this earth, not in this life. I know it, but I must not think of it. There is Paris still to take. There is still God's work to be done, and I must be about it. I must go to the king. We must take Paris at once. There must be no delay.'

But there was nothing but delay. The new King Charles, basking in the glory of his coronation, strutted about his court like a puffed up peacock. 'Patience, Joan,' he told her. 'If things go my way, we shall take Paris without ever lifting a sword.'

'How?' Joan demanded.

And the king, surrounded as he was by La Trémoille and his friends, all of them deeply envious of Joan and only too happy to see her thwarted, put his arm around her, and said cryptically: 'You will see, Joan. You will see.'

For days on end the king would say nothing more, and then at last he summoned her to him. He was waving a scroll at her as she came in. 'You see Joan? I have it. I have it from the Duke of Burgundy himself. Peace. I have his word, his promise. In fifteen days he will surrender Paris to us. What do you think of that?'

'I think it is a trick,' Joan replied. 'You have been ill advised, Charles. Ask yourself why he should ask for fifteen days if it is not to reinforce his garrison with English soldiers. You have been fooled, and not only by the Duke of Burgundy, but by La Trémoille and your own advisers, too. I tell you truly that neither the Duke of Burgundy nor his English masters will come to terms unless it be to their own advantage. Like it or not, we shall have to drive them out. I do not wish for war, nor certainly for bloodshed, but the lance and the sword are all they understand. This treaty, my lord king, is not worth the paper it is written on. I spit upon the Duke of Burgundy and upon his treaty, too.'

And with that she stormed out. The Duc d'Alençon hurried after her.

'You will make dangerous enemies, Joan,' he warned her.

She wheeled round to face him. 'Am I right or am I not?'

'You are right,' d'Alençon conceded.

'Well then. And I care not a fig for my enemies. If they are my enemies then they are the enemies of my king and my country. Your enemies, too, my fair duke.'

'But they could harm you, Joan.'

'I know it, and no doubt they will try. But meanwhile I would have the army out in the field and ready to march.' She put an arm on his.

'See to it for me, d'Alençon. We must take Paris. If we do not, I tell you, we are lost.' Belami flew down at that moment and landed on d'Alençon's shoulder.

'He's never done that before,' d'Alençon laughed.

'Maybe he trusts you,' said Joan, 'as I do.'

Within a few days it was clear that Joan had been right all along. English soldiers under the Duke of Bedford were reported to be pouring into Paris. Even knowing this the king dithered and would not move against him, but waited until the fifteen days of the treaty were up. Only then did he grudgingly allow the Duc d'Alençon and Joan to move on Paris.

From St Denis outside Paris, Joan rode out to reconnoitre the defences. The walls were higher, the ditches under the moats deeper than at Orléans, deeper than she had ever seen before. She rode back in silence with d'Alençon.

'You know it cannot be done, Joan,' he said at last.

'It must be done,' she replied. 'And I shall do it. In God's name I shall do it. The sight of us coming will be enough on its own. The city will rise in our support.'

'Do your voices tell you this?' d'Alençon asked.

For a moment she was silent. 'No,' she said. 'My voices have not spoken to me for some time now. I hate it when they are silent. I am so alone without them.'

'You have me, Joan,' said d'Alençon. 'You will always have me.'

'Nothing and no one is for always,' Joan replied. 'Everything and everyone has its end. Only God is eternal. We must not forget that.' She reined in her horse and surveyed the walls of Paris. 'Tomorrow, with God's blessing, I shall say Mass in Paris.'

But she did not say Mass in Paris the next day, nor any other day; neither did the populace rise in her support as she had hoped. Attack after attack was driven off. But in spite of all d'Alençon's pleadings, Joan would not hear of retreat. Whenever they saw her standard raised her army would rally again. Wherever she led, they would follow – many, so many, to their deaths. When she was herself wounded in the thigh by an arrow, Louis, her brothers and Richard the Archer had to drag her protesting to safety. 'We can try again tomorrow, if you like, Joan,' said d'Alençon. 'But for today it is enough. You must rest. The army must rest.'

That night, at Joan's command and under cover of darkness, the Duc d'Alençon built a wooden bridge across the ditch near St Denis for a surprise attack the next morning; but unknown either to d'Alençon or Joan a terrible treachery was afoot. Before morning came the bridge had mysteriously caught fire. The attack had to be called off. For days, as Joan lay recovering in her tent, the army could only sit and watch the walls of Paris. Despite all Joan's best endeavours to persuade the king there were no new assaults. Whispers about the camp told the story, a story Joan found quite impossible to believe when she first heard it. But when her brothers confirmed it, and d'Alençon too, then she had to believe it. King Charles himself, it seemed, the king she had restored to his throne, had personally ordered the bridge to be destroyed, and the attack on Paris to be halted. Behind her back he had come to terms again with the Burgundians and the English. Paris and the north of the country would be left to the Duke of Burgundy and the English, if he could keep all the conquests to the south. The king was going to disband his army, her army, leaving the English still in France. She wept when she heard it, more in anger than in sorrow.

❖

CHAPTER EIGHT

Alone in the Wilderness

Confirmation of her king's treachery was not long in coming. He summoned her to him, and told her abruptly that he had run out of money. He could not afford to continue the siege of Paris, he said. He was disbanding the army, and she must accompany him and his court back to the Loire. The campaign was over.

'You are God's anointed King of all France,' she told him, 'and so I must obey you.' And looking hard at La Trémoille and the king's advisers, she went on. 'You serve neither your king, nor your country but only yourselves. What you have done you will live to regret, I promise you.' And sweeping them with a gaze of undisguised contempt, she left them.

Filled with anger and disgust she went at once to the cathedral of St Denis, where she pulled off her armour and hurled it to the ground by the tombs of the French kings. D'Alençon found her praying there some time later, Belami perched nearby. D'Alençon knelt beside. He could see she was in tears.

'Such a man is not worth crying for, Joan,' he said. 'Such a man should not be king.'

'Do not speak ill of him,' she replied. 'He is our king. God's annointed. I am crying for France, not for him. I shall go on fighting for France till the end, whatever the end may be. My king will not stop me. None of them will.' She turned to him. 'As for you, my fair duke, you have done all you can. No man has been a greater friend to me. But the rest I must do on my own. My voices tell me so.'

'They have spoken to you again?'

'Just now,' she said. 'As I was praying. Like my Lord in Heaven, like Jesus himself, they say I must be alone in the wilderness a while, and only after that shall we have a final victory. They have promised it. So I must send you away, back home to your wife, as I promised I would.' D'Alençon tried to protest, but he could see how determined she was.

'Go now,' she said, getting to her feet and embracing him fondly.

'Will I ever see you again?' he asked, her hands in his.

'God willing,' she replied. And he walked away and left her there alone amongst the tombs, her armour scattered all around her feet.

For Joan the wilderness was not the wilderness of the desert but the wilderness of loneliness, of boredom. For months she trailed loyally round after her indolent king and his court of sycophants, from castle to castle, from town to town, his tame warrior saint, to be shown off like some prize exhibit. All the time she begged to be allowed to attack Paris again, or to drive the English out of Normandy, but neither the king nor La Trémoille would agree to it. In her despair she talked more and more to Belami. To her brothers, to Louis, she betrayed none of her deepest fears, none of her growing doubts. Only to Belami. 'The blessed St Margaret and St Catherine tell me that all shall be well, that I shall soon have my army again; but they do not say when, nor why I must wait. Be patient, they say. But how long must I be patient, Belami, how long? Oh Belami, they would not deceive me, would they? Would they? I must not even think it.'

By the spring, the king and La Trémoille had to accept that the Duke of Burgundy was playing them false, for even they could see that the Burgundians and English were breaking the treaty at will. He sent for Joan, who came at once.

'I want you to frighten them for me, Joan,' he said. 'To remind them who is the rightful King of France, I want you to remind them of what you did at Orléans, at Patay. That should make them keep their treaties. I cannot give you many men, Joan, but ten Frenchmen behind your standard are worth a thousand traitorous Burgundians, two thousand English Godoms.'

With great joy Joan set out again on her campaign. News spread quickly that Joan the Maid was on the march again. She had only a small force, but it was enough, to begin with. Towns rose spontaneously in rebellion against their Burgundian masters, against their English occupiers. One such town was Melun, where the citizens opened the gates to greet their Joan, their liberator.

Belami flew off to drink down by the river. When he returned he found Joan leaning out over the ramparts, looking at the sunset. He landed beside her. 'I shall be taken prisoner, Belami,' she whispered. 'The blessed St Margaret has just told me so. I must not be surprised, she says. It is necessary for this to happen, she says. I must accept it with good grace. God will help me. God will help me. Oh I hope so. If they take me, Belami, I'd rather be killed. I told her that, Belami. I want to be killed, I do not want to be their prisoner. I begged her, but she made me no reply. Oh may God preserve me.' And she put her head on her arms and wept bitterly.

Belami came nearer to comfort her, but she would not be comforted. The sun had gone down leaving the world black and cold about them before Joan raised her head again. She touched Belami tenderly. 'Oh, Belami,' she said, 'what must be, must be. I must put it from my mind entirely, or I shall not be able to fight as I must. Stay with me, Belami, whatever happens, please stay with me.'

Perhaps it was the months of enforced idleness, or maybe it was the knowledge that her time was short, but Joan lost no opportunity now to attack the English and Burgundians whenever she could. She moved towards Compiègne, a town loyal to the king and being threatened by both the English under the Duke of Bedford and the Burgundians. Her daring and her dash inspired her small army to great feats of courage, often attacking much greater forces that stood in their way. But she missed the companionship of d'Alençon and the support of La Hire. She was general now, and captain and standard bearer too. It was a heavy burden. They cut a swathe though enemy country, reaching Compiègne at last after a lightning march through the forest.

Once in the town, Joan rested only briefly, then sallied out that same evening to spy out the land, Belami flying overhead. She would have to cross the bridge over the river. Behind her there were archers on the walls covering her retreat and men with crossbows in boats in case of ambush. Joan had always been daring, but never reckless, until now. When she saw enemy, she attacked at once; but suddenly there were more of them, and then more still, charging at her out of the trees. Before she knew it she found herself surrounded. They fought their way back to the bridge, towards the drawbridge, her brothers, Louis and Richard the Archer alongside her. It was no one's fault. They thought everyone was safe inside and pulled the drawbridge up. Everyone was safe, except Joan and Richard the Archer who was struck down as he tried to defend her.

Joan was alone now amongst her enemies. They were tugging on her horse's bridle. Then rough hands were dragging her off to the ground, and manhandling her back across the bridge and into captivity. She looked up at the sky and saw Belami. 'Fly Belami,' she cried. 'Fly.' Just the sight of him up there and flying free gave her new courage. 'You cannot cage me,' she cried, kicking and struggling against them.

'Cage you?' laughed one of her captors, 'We're not going to cage you, Joan. We're going to burn you. We burn witches, don't we?'

Within hours of her capture she was led before the Duke of Burgundy himself. She looked him hard in the eye, a look that stared deep into his soul and troubled him.

'They say you will burn me,' she said.

'Not I,' said the Duke. 'I'll not have your death on my hands. No, I'll sell you to the English. I'll let them do my dirty work for me.'

'Have you forgotten my king?' cried Joan. 'Do you think he would stand by and let you sell me to the English?'

'Which king do you speak of? Your King in Heaven or the knock-kneed imbecile you crowned at Reims?'

'Both. My King in Heaven will protect me. He has promised us victory over you and the English, and so sooner or later we shall have it. And my king on this earth will either pay you more than the English or come to my rescue. Either way you will not hold me long.'

The duke, stirred to sudden anger, pulled out his dagger and would have plunged it into her heart then but for the restraining arm of Jean of Luxembourg. 'Leave her with me, my lord duke. I shall take her to my castle at Beaurevoir. We can keep her there as long as you like, until the price is right. English, French – no matter – she's worth a fortune to us alive. Very little if she's dead.'

'Very well,' said the duke, sheathing his dagger. 'In the meantime I shall take Compiègne and put every man and woman in the town to the sword. Now they have none of her devilish powers to protect them any more, they will soon surrender. Take her to Beaurevoir then. But if she escapes, Jean, I shall have your head.'

So Joan was taken to Beaurevoir, a fine castle overlooking the River Escaut. Unnoticed, of course, Belami went with her, from rooftop to chimney, from hedgerow to tree, never far out of her sight, and then at last flew in the window of the high tower where she was held.

In those first weeks of captivity Joan was as well looked after as she could possibly have hoped for. Burgundian in his sentiments though he was, Jean of Luxembourg was honoured to have her as his prisoner and treated her more like an important guest. They may have fought one another, but he admired her courage and wondered at how a peasant girl from Lorraine could have beaten them on the field of battle so soundly and for so long. Secretly, like many others, he relished her victories over the arrogant English. Burgundian allies they might have been, but they were not much liked.

Secure in her tower Joan was at last amongst women, Jean of Luxembourg's wife, and his aunt and stepdaughter. In the circumstances they could not have been kinder. They did try to persuade Joan to change out of her men's clothes, and even made her a dress, white with embroidered wild roses. It fitted perfectly, but still Joan would not put it on. 'I thank you but I may not,' she told them. 'My voices have forbidden it. I am a soldier, you see.'

If it were ever possible to be happy and be a captive at the same time, then Joan achieved this at Beaurevoir. She had her Belami beside her. She had gentle, kindly women to attend on her. She could say Mass whenever she wanted Yet still she was restless and troubled. Those last threatening words of the Duke of Burgundy – how he would butcher everyone in Compiègne, how the English would burn her – echoed in her head. And worse, as time passed, she did begin to wonder why it was that her king had not yet sent an army to rescue her, nor had she any news that he had even tried to pay her ransom.

'I will not be taken by the English, Belami.' She would often say it when they were alone. 'I would rather die first. My king wouldn't let it happen. He wouldn't, would he Belami? Would he?' But the more she asked the question, the more she doubted the answer. She prayed for hours on end for guidance, but her voices told her nothing, only that she must be patient. She began to despair. 'But the more I am patient and the longer I wait,' she told Belami one night, 'the more I know that my king has deserted me. Where is he? Where is La Hire? Where is my fair d'Alençon, and Jean and Bertrand? Have they all abandoned me, Belami, all my friends? Well, I will not abandon the people of Compiègne. They need me. The people of France need me. Here I can do nothing. I shall wait no longer, despite all my voices tell me. I must leave here, Belami. I cannot fight my way out – there are soldiers everywhere. So I will do what you do, Belami. I will fly. My voices have forbidden it, but I must do it in spite of them. In this I must disobey them. And you will be with me, won't you Belami?'

Belami was there at dawn the next day as she crept out of her room and out on to the roof. He flew frantically around her beating his wings against her head, trying to stop her. 'I will not look down,' she said. 'I must not.' She crossed herself, commended herself to God and jumped.

As she lay senseless and still on the grass, one leg twisted underneath her, blood coming from her mouth, Belami was quite sure she was dead. So were the soldiers when they found her some minutes later and carried her up into the castle. But when they laid her out on the bed they found she was still breathing. By the time the ladies had finished bathing her, her eyes had opened. She sat up and looked about her, bewildered, but only for a moment. 'Ah,' she cried, and fell back again, weeping pitifully. 'So I am still a prisoner. I have lost my best chance, my only hope.' To begin with she refused to eat, and wanted only to die but the ladies insisted. Two days later she had recovered almost completely. She limped a little on her swollen ankle, but otherwise she was quite unharmed. The doctor who examined her could not believe what he saw. 'It's a miracle,' he told Jean of Luxembourg. 'She should be dead. The angels held her up. The angels saved her.'

'Where she is going,' said Jean of Luxembourg sadly, 'I fear they will not call them angels. They will call them devils.'

'What do you mean?' asked his wife. He told them then what he dreaded telling them: that Pierre Cauchon, Bishop of Beauvais and a staunch ally of the English, was already on his way to Beaurevoir; that a deal had been struck. The English would pay ten thousand pounds for Joan. They were the masters in France. He had no choice but to accept. 'Any day now Cauchon will be here,' he said. 'God only knows what the English will do to her.'

'Poor girl,' said his wife. 'Poor, poor girl. How they will make her suffer.'

When Joan first heard she was to be delivered into the hands of the Bishop, that she was to be taken to Rouen, to be tried in a church court, that her judges were to be bishops and priors and abbots, she cried for joy. 'Then I am safe, Belami, safe. For no court of priests would condemn me for loving God, for doing his will, and that is all I have done, all I have ever done.'

She thought it strange, though, when she left Beaurevoir on her long journey to Rouen that her guards were English soldiers, stranger still that they chained her each night like a dog. Strange became ominous when the Bishop of Beauvais would not look her in the eye, would not answer her questions, and when he would not allow her to say Mass nor have a priest to confess to. Gone were the niceties of her time at Beaurevoir. Surrounded now entirely by men, rough men who took pleasure in mocking her and abusing her, who allowed her little or no privacy, Joan took refuge in defiant silence. Now she knew. She didn't need to be told what they intended for her. The English had bought her. The Church would try her and condemn her if they could. Then hand her over to the English for burning. In the depths of night when her guards were asleep she would sit in the corner of whatever dark dungeon they had thrown her into and wait for Belami to come to her. She knew that Belami would find a way to get to her and he almost always did. Through Crotoy, Arras and Dieppe, they took her. Belami was with her all the time. If ever they were alone, she would talk to him, open her heart to him. 'It is as I said it would be, Belami, just you and me now. I shall not weaken, Belami, I shall not cry in front of them, no matter what they do, what they say. My voices speak to me all the time now, Belami – the Blessed St Margaret, the Blessed St Catherine – they will not desert me. France will be free of the enemy, they have promised it. And all will be well for me. They have promised me that, too. And what they have promised has always come to pass. Only when I get above myself and do not listen to my voices, only then, do I come to grief – when I attacked Paris, remember? Or when I jumped from my tower at Beaurevoir. They have told me they will help me through my ordeal. They will find a way for me. They have promised it.' She sighed as she stroked him.' How I miss Louis, and my fair d'Alençon, and my dear brothers and my mother and my father, and Hauviette. How I miss Hauviette. You know, Belami, I have almost forgotten what she looks like. It's as if I knew her in another life.'

With every mile they took her further from her family, further from her friends, and even deeper into English occupied territory. Here too she was known, but here no one cheered her. No one called out blessings. No one smiled. When at last they brought her that cold December to Rouen, they paraded her bound through the streets, streets crowded with Burgundians and English taunting her, swearing at her, spitting at her. Joan could ignore their hateful eyes, their vicious innuendoes and insults. She only had to look up at Belami flying ahead of her and she would soar with him above the horror of it all.

She had some hopes at first that she might be kept amongst nuns in a church prison during her trial, that she might now be kept away from the leering eyes of her English captors. But her hopes were soon dashed. She found herself cast into a cell where the walls ran with damp, where rats scuttled across the floor. She had no bed, but was chained around her body night and day to a great log of wood. Worse, there were the same English guards to contend with, their bestial eyes and their

grasping hands. She thanked God she had on her men's clothes, that she was bedraggled and filthy. That, with her steely defiance, was all that could protect her now.

But even here she was not entirely without hope. Belami could fly in through the tiny window to be with her. She had her Belami and she had her God.

Many of the great lords and dukes of England – Warwick, Bedford, Stafford and others – came to see her in her cell, sometimes even bringing their wives with them. They came mostly to gloat; but once there, once they saw her wretched state and her heroic courage in the face of all her hardships and in the face of what they knew to be her impending fate, they could gloat no more. She stood before them in her chains unbowed and calm, her eyes ablaze with defiance. Even if they hated her, even if they wanted her dead – and many of them did – they saw her with new and grudging respect.

Jean of Luxembourg came time and again, sent by his wife, to try to help Joan save herself. 'I will ransom you,' he told her. 'The English will allow it, but only if you promise never to take up arms against them or us ever again.'

Always she gave him the same reply. 'They think by killing me they will have all of France for themselves. But I tell you, even if there were a hundred thousand Godoms more than there are now, they should not have the kingdom. I will make you no such promises. Let them have their trial. I will answer them truthfully as my voices have told me I should. I am not afraid. I will never be afraid.' It was not said as a boast, rather as a promise to herself, for there was a terror deep inside her that she felt might one day make a coward of her.

CHAPTER NINE

Trial and Tribulation

 It wasn't until the end of February that they led her at last to her trial, barefoot and bound in chains, to the chapel Royal in the castle at Rouen. She was wracked with fever as she sat down at last to face her judges: the bloated, bulbous figure of Pierre Cauchon, Bishop of Beauvais, and either side of him a dozen abbots and priors – grim, grey men with hard eyes and thin lips. And evident in all of them, as they looked into her eyes, was the presumption of her guilt. They had made up their minds. They had judged her already. She knew it for sure when they read out a letter from the King of England commanding the bishop to have her tried. She knew well enough what else he was commanding, unspoken, unwritten though it was. They were to condemn her as a heretic, as a witch, and have her burnt. But Joan had her voices. Somehow she would be saved. All will be well, they had told her. Sure in her faith, she would fight her accusers, fight them to the last, not with swords any more, but with words.

High above her, Belami sat on a rafter and watched and listened to it all. It had taken a while to find a hole in the chapel roof, but he was sure he would find one. He'd never yet known a roof without one. Weakened by her long captivity, Joan had only strength enough to speak softly, but like everyone else he heard every word she said.

Through it all, Cauchon fixed his eyes on her, like a stoat before a kill. He would lean forward and do his utmost to mesmerize her, to cower her; but Joan outfaced him, she outfaced all of them. She stood accused of sorcery, of blasphemy, of witchcraft. Hour after hour they interrogated her, day after day, week after week; first in the Chapel Royal but later they came to her cell in the castle. Through it all, often sick with cold and fatigue, Joan answered them the only way she knew – with the truth as she saw it, as she remembered it. She hid from them only what her voices had said she should.

Her judges tried to confuse her, to bewilder her, lulling her with smiles and seemingly simple, straightforward questions. But every question, no matter how simple, hid an accusation, and Joan knew it. Exhausted as she was, she countered them each time, bore all their bullying, all their threats, even finding the strength to laugh at them sometimes, and chide them. They hoped to wear her into submission, to beat her down, so that she would confess either that she had invented her voices, or that they came from the devil himself and therefore she must be a witch. But she would not be intimidated. Even when they took her to the torture chamber so that she could see for herself how terrible the instruments were, she would not confess. She told them they could do their worst, she was not afraid. She had spoken the truth and would not be deflected from it, not by torture, nor by the fire.

From his perch on the chapel rafters and from the window of her cell, Belami witnessed every moment of it.

Unlike Joan, he heard how, once she had been led away, her judges seethed with frustration and fury at their failure yet again to browbeat her into submission. He saw how Pierre Cauchon bent them all to his will, how before each interrogation he would conspire with them to devise some new way to unsettle her and break her at last.

The questions came fast, one upon the other, from different judges, about her childhood, her voices, her men's clothes, her miracles, leaving her little time to think or to consider her answers carefully, each judge seeking to trick her into some weakness, some inconsistency that might betray her.

'What age were you when you left your father's house?'
'I cannot remember.'
'What age were you when your voices came for the first time?'
'Thirteen.'
'What teaching do your voices give you?'
'They taught me how to behave.'
'Who advised you to take male dress?'
'My voices.'
'When you found King Charles at Chinon, how did you recognize him?'
'By the advice of my voices.'
'When did you last eat?'
'Yesterday afternoon.'

'When did you last hear your voices?'

'Yesterday and today.'

'What were you doing when you last heard your voices?'

'I was asleep. The voices woke me.'

'Did they touch you?'

'No.'

'Is the voice of an angel or does it come from God?'

'It comes from God.'

'Do you believe you are in the grace of God?'

'If I am not, may God put me there. If I am, may He keep me there. If I am not in His grace, then I would be the most miserable person in the world.'

'Did you play in the fields with the other children when you were young?'

'Sometimes.'

'Did you play at fights, English against French, with the other children?'

'No, so far as I can remember, but I saw my friends fighting with the children of Maxey. I saw them coming home wounded and bleeding.'

'When you were young, did you have a great desire to defeat the Burgundians?'

'I had a great desire that the king should have his kingdom.'

'Do you want a woman's dress?'

'I am content with what I have, since it is God's will I wear it.'

'Does it seem to you lawful to wear a man's dress?'

'Everything done at Our Lord's command must be well done, must be lawful.'

'The sword found at Fierbois, how did you know it was behind the altar?'

'My voices. They said it would be in the ground, all rusted, with five crosses upon it.'

'Which do you prefer, your sword or your standard?'

'I am forty times fonder of my standard than I am of the sword.'

'Who persuaded you to have "Jhesus Maria" embroidered on your standard?'

'I have told you often enough. I have done nothing except by God's command.'

'At Orléans, did you know beforehand that you would be wounded?'

'Yes, I did. And I tell you, before seven years are past, the English will have lost more than Orléans. They will lose all they hold in France.'

'How do you know this?'

'Through St Catherine and St Margaret.'

'Do they always appear to you in the same form?'

'Always, their heads richly crowned.'

'What part of the saints do you see?'

'The face.'

'Do they have hair?'

'Of course.'

'How do they speak?'

'Sweet and low in tone. And they speak in French.'

'Do they not speak in English?'

'Why should they? They are not on the English side, are they?'

'What about St Michael? What clothes does he have?'

'I can't remember.'

'Is he naked?'

'Do you think Our Lord has not the wherewithal to clothe him?'

'Do your voices say you will escape?'

'They tell me I shall be delivered. But I know neither the day nor the hour. God's will be done.'

'Where did you first put on a man's dress?'

'Vaucouleurs.'

'Do those on your side firmly believe you are sent by God?'

'I don't know if they believe it. But if they do not believe it, still I am sent from God.'

'Did your voices tell you you would be taken prisoner?'

'Yes, almost every day they told me. I asked only that I should die speedily without suffering a long imprisonment.'

'Did you have the world and two angels embroidered on your standard?'

'Yes.'

'What significance is there in that?'

'St Catherine and St Margaret said it should be made in this fashion, that I should bear it boldly and to have painted upon it the King of Heaven.'

'Did you do well in leaving home without the permission of your mother and father, seeing that you should honour your mother and father?'

'I was in everything most obedient to them, save in this departure.'

'Did you not commit a sin in leaving your mother and father like that?'

'Since God commanded it, I had to obey. If I'd had a hundred fathers and mothers, if I'd been a king's daughter, I would still have gone.'

'Did you do wrong in wearing a man's dress?'

'No.'

'Did you leap from the tower at Beaurevoir on the advice of your voices?'

'Almost every day St. Catherine told me not to leap, that God would help me and the people of Compiègne.'

'When you leapt did you expect to kill yourself?'

'No, I entrusted myself to God and hoped that by means of this leap I could escape and avoid being handed over to the English.'

'Have you asked God's permission to escape from prison?'

'I have often asked for it, but so far have not had it. But If I saw an open door I would go, for this would be Our Lord's permission.'

In those very words the questions came at her and in those very words she answered them. Time and again she begged to be able to say Mass. They refused her. She asked to be released from her chains. They refused her. She asked not to be left with the soldiers. They refused her.

Even inside her cell she was never alone. There were always three English soldiers in there with her and two outside on guard. But in the dead of night when they were all asleep, Belami would fly in and perch on her shoulder. She could not even move her hand to stroke him now for fear of rattling her chains and waking the guards. But she could turn her head to see him. In the intimate privacy of the dark she would weep her silent tears, and share with Belami her most dread doubts and fearful terrors. As the trial came at last towards its end and the hour of the inevitable verdict came closer, she was ever more haunted by the horror of the death she would soon have to endure.

'I fear the heat of the flames, Belami,' she whispered, 'but I fear my fear more. My voices tell me that I must endure all, that I must not weaken. But all I have to do is confess that my voices were false, throw myself on the mercy of the Church and obey them in everything, and I could still save myself. And I so want to save myself. I so want to live. I am young. But I must not weaken now, Belami, I must not. When I die in the flames it will be quickly over, won't it? And afterwards I will be in Paradise forever, won't I? Won't I? Stay by me tomorrow when they judge me, Belami. Stay by me.'

It was many weeks now since Joan had seen the light of day. It was a beautiful May morning as they led her, still manacled, to the walled cemetery behind the abbey. The brightness of the sun dazzled and hurt her eyes.

'A fine day for a burning,' cried someone from the crowd.

'Burn the witch,' they cried. 'Burn her! Burn her! To the stake with her! To the stake!'

CHAPTER TEN

Where Shall
I be Tonight?

Swallows and swifts swooped and screamed over the rooftops and reminded her of home, of Domrémy, and summers when she was little. A tide of sadness threatened to overwhelm her utterly. And then white amongst the swallows and hovering like a lark, she saw Belami. 'Dear Belami,' she breathed. 'Dear faithful Belami.'

The cemetery was crowded with all manner of people, soldiers, merchants, priests, nuns, restless now with expectancy as she mounted her stand; Master Erard, one of the court's many lawyers – she had had no lawyer to defend her all through the trial – was at her elbow. On another stand opposite were ranged her accusers. She counted five bishops, Cauchon amongst them, priors, abbots, and behind them the English lords, Warwick and Stafford, watching over it all.

A hush fell as Master Erard began his speech. It was a long speech and Joan was faint from the heat of the sun and had to clutch the rail to stop herself from falling. That was when she first saw below her the executioner's cart, waiting. She saw the upturned faces of the crowd, watching her, hating her, longing to see her burn. Master Erard ranted on at her, berating her for all her wickedness, listing all her crimes and iniquities, all the charges against her. When he had finished, everyone waited for her answer.

She spoke out firmly so that all could hear her. 'I have already told you that everything I have done, I have done at God's command.'

At this Cauchon rose from his seat and began at once to pronounce the sentence on her.

'Then we declare you excommunicate and heretical and pronounce you shall be abandoned to secular justice, as a limb of Satan severed from the Church. . .' As Joan listened, still reeling in her stand, she saw the executioner's horse tossing his head impatiently. She saw the cruel smile on the executioner's face. She could bear it no more.

'I submit,' she cried, 'I confess it all. My voices were false to me. All I did, I did against the laws of God and Holy Mother Church. I submit myself to the Church, to the mercy of you, my judges. I do not believe my voices, nor in my apparitions. I made them up. I pretended it all. I confess it. I will do whatever you desire, whatever the Church desires. Only not the fire. Please, not the fire.'

For a moment the crowd were stunned to silence, aghast at what they had just heard. They had come to see Joan burnt as a witch, not to witness her recantation, not to see her escape at the last moment. During the fearful pandemonium that followed, someone thrust a paper into her hand, and told her to sign. She could see nothing but the executioner's cart. She would have signed anything. 'But I cannot write,' she cried.

'Make your mark then,' said Master Erard. And he took her hand and helped her mark the document with a trembling cross. Then he flourished it in triumph above his head and then he read it out loud, straining to make himself heard against all the jeering of the crowd. They scarcely heard a word of it. But Joan did.

'She has signed. The Maid has signed,' Erard began. 'Here it is. Here it is. "I, Joan, called The Maid, a miserable sinner, after I recognized the snare of error in which I was held; and now that I have by God's grace, returned to Our Mother Holy Church; I do confess that I have grievously sinned in falsely pretending that I have had revelations from God and his angels, St Catherine and St Margaret, etc . . . All my words and deeds which are contrary to the Church, I do revoke; and I desire to live in unity with the Church, nevermore departing therefrom. In witness whereof my sign manual." And see, she makes her mark with this cross.'

As she listened, Joan hung her head and cried bitterly. Through her tears she looked down at the seething crowd below her, lusting for her death. They were shaking their fists at her, cursing her, screaming at her.

'Witch! Slut! Fiend! Harlot! Whore!' She put her hands over her ears and closed her eyes to shut it all out.

By the time she opened them again, Cauchon had almost finished pronouncing her new sentence. 'Wherefore we have condemned you to perpetual imprisonment with the bread of sorrow and the water of affliction that you may weep for your sins and never more commit them.'

'Take me, then, to your church prison,' she cried, 'so that I may no longer be in the hands of these English.'

But Cauchon simply said, 'Take her back where she has come from.'

Belami was there at the window of her cell when Cauchon and other priests came that evening to see her.

'The Church has dealt kindly with you, Joan,' said Cauchon. 'Learn humility, learn obedience. Leave all your revelations and stupidities behind you. If you do not then you cannot count on our protection and we will be forced to hand you over to the English. You do understand that, Joan?'

'Yes, my lord bishop. But may I say Mass? May I be released of my chains?'

'If you will at once leave off your men's clothes and henceforth wear only women's clothes. Your boy's hair will be shorn.'

That night, her head shorn, and wearing women's clothes for the first time since she left Vaucouleurs two years before, Joan sat and endured the coarse jibes of her guards. Her men's clothes lay in a heap in the corner of the cell.

There was no sleep for Joan that night.

Belami came to her whenever he could, but it could not be so often. She was ever more closely guarded now, and one guard seemed always to be awake.

Joan sat all the while, unmoving and staring into space. Belami waited till the moment was right, till the guards were distracted, and landed behind her, where he could not be seen. It was nothing then to flutter up and perch, hidden behind her shoulder. 'What I have done today, Belami, I should not have done,' she whispered. 'So I will undo it. I will. I'll make you proud of me again, Belami, that much I promise you. I will try again to be brave, I will try.'

The next day the judges were called to the prison. They found Joan dressed once more in her man's clothes and refusing to change back.

'Why have you done this?' Cauchon asked.

'Because being with men it is more convenient and more suitable. Because you have not allowed me to say Mass as I asked, nor to have my irons removed.'

'Have you heard your voices again, Joan?' the Bishop asked her.

'Yes. They have told me what I ought to do, and I'm doing it.'

'So you claim again that these are the voices of saints, of St Catherine and St Margaret?'

'Yes.'

'What did they say to you?'

'They told me that in saving my life I was damning myself, that if I were to say that God had not sent me, then I should be damning myself, for it is true that God did send me. My voices have told me that I did very wrong in doing all I did. It was only the fear of the fire which made me say what I said.'

'Out of your own mouth you have condemned yourself to the fire,' said Cauchon.

'I know it,' Joan replied. 'Let it come swiftly. But before it happens let me say my confession. Let me have a last communion. And no chains, for once, no chains. It is all I ask.'

As Cauchon looked down at her, he felt for her for the first time and pitied her.

'I should not allow it,' he said, 'but I shall.'

She spent her last night on earth sitting with Belami in her lap, just as she had done when she first found him all those years before. She said little, but stroked him constantly. At dawn she took him to the window. 'When it is over, Belami, go back to Domrémy. Hauviette will look after you.'

She took communion in her cell and made her confession to Brother Martin, looking to him for a last reassurance.

'Where shall I be tonight?' she asked.

'Have you no faith in Our Lord?' he replied.

'Yes, God helping me. Today I shall be with Him in Paradise.'

They came for her at once and took her out, still in her chains, to the market square. There must have been ten thousand people waiting there, faces at every window, children clinging to chimney pots. There was a platform for the judges, a platform for the priests, and in the centre a scaffold with a great stake piled all

around with wood. And in front of the stake was a board, with writing printed on it for all to read: 'Joan, who called herself The Maid, liar, pernicious, deceiver of the people, sorceress, superstitious, blasphemer of God, presumptuous, disbeliever in the faith of Jesus Christ, boastful, idolatrous, cruel, dissolute, invoker of devils, apostate and heretic.'

They led her first up on to the platform where the priests stood, Cauchon amongst them. Many of them were in tears. Here she knelt and prayed aloud, beseeching God to show her mercy and to forgive her judges for all they had done to her. When she had finished Cauchon read out the sentence of death.

'Since you, Joan, have been found by us relapsed into diverse errors and crimes and wickednesses, as a dog returns to its vomit, we do cast you forth and eject you from the communion of the Church as an infected limb, and hand you over to secular justice.' The rest was drowned in a great cheer as Joan was dragged down the steps and across the market square towards the scaffold. Rough hands bound her to the stake. One English soldier stuck a paper hat on her head, and spat in her face. On the hat he had scrawled: 'Heretic. Relapsed. Apostate. Idolatress.'

Already the executioner had his torch alight. But then, just as he lit the fire, another English soldier sprang up on to the faggots, a wooden cross in his hand.

115

He held it to her lips so she might kiss it. She looked into his face to thank him and saw, under the English helmet, that it was Louis; her page and friend. 'God bless you, sweet Joan,' he said.

'Get down,' she cried. 'They are lighting the fire.'

But Louis stayed till the very last moment, with the smoke rising now through the faggots, he sprang back to safety just in time, stumbled backwards and fell. By the time he looked up again the flames were all around her. . .

'Jesus! Jesus!' she cried, and then her head fell forward and she never spoke again. All that could be heard was the crackle of the flames.

There were no cheers now. Many cried openly at what they had just witnessed. 'We are lost,' said one of the English soldiers. 'We have just burnt a saint.'

Another soldier standing close to Louis, gripped his arm suddenly, and pointed. 'Look,' he cried. 'A white dove flying up out of the fire. It's her soul. It's a miracle, a miracle.'

But Louis could see well enough that the bird rising from the smoke was no dove, but a white sparrow and one he knew well. Belami hovered for some moments over the square, then flew off back home, back to Domrémy. Louis watched him until he could see him no more.

CHAPTER ELEVEN

The Sparrow and the Saint

 I woke, and looked about me. Somehow I expected Jaquot to be there, but he was not. There was no sparrow to be seen, no bird at all in the sky above me, only a plane flying high, silver in the sun, a vapour trail blossoming in its wake.

I glanced down at my watch. I had been all day down by the river, yet it seemed to have passed so quickly. School would be over by now. I could go back home as if I'd been at school all day long. No one would know the difference.

At supper that evening my mother and father were prattling on and on about my birthday the next day, about how birthdays seem more important every year you get older, then about how they were pleased to be the age they were, how they wouldn't want to be seventeen again, even if they could be. They were being kind. They were simply avoiding any mention of the Joan of Arc celebrations the next day. I was hardly listening

'Good day at school, Eloise?' my father asked me. I was caught completely unawares. I had no reply. Luckily for me the phone rang. My father picked it up.

'Yes. Hello, yes. She's home now, yes . . . You mean this evening? All right. I'll tell her then. Goodbye.' He put the phone down.

'What?' asked my mother.

He was pouring himself some wine. 'Her again,' he said. 'Friend of yours from school, Eloise – Marie Duval. She wants to see you. She's coming round.'

My mother turned to me. 'Oh, we didn't tell you, did we? She called earlier, came to the door. She said she was looking for you at school today. Couldn't seem to find you anywhere. No one could, she said. Funny, that.'

I looked down at my plate and wished the floor would just open up and swallow me.

'Where did you get to, Eloise?' my mother asked. 'Where have you been? I've been worried sick. I mean really worried.'

'The river,' I replied, not looking up from my plate. 'I went down to the river.

I just couldn't go to school. Not today. I couldn't face it. I'm sorry.'

I couldn't eat another thing. I was close to tears and they knew better than to talk to me. My mind roamed from one thing to another, from Jaquot by the river to Belami and Joan in the garden at Domrémy, to Joan burning in Rouen, to Marie Duval. Why was she coming? What for? Back to Joan again, Joan storming the Tourelles, Joan praying by the river at Orléans, Jaquot by the river at Orléans.

The door bell rang.

It was strange seeing Marie Duval in my house. There were a few awkward introductions in the hall. Then I took her out into the garden so that we could be alone.

'I looked for you at school,' she began. I said nothing. I didn't want to have to explain. 'Well, it's about tomorrow,' she went on. 'The parade, the procession, whatever they call it.'

'What about it?' I asked.

'The thing is,' she said, 'I read it. I read your essay on Joan of Arc. Everyone's read it. They pinned it up at school this morning – it's coming out in the newspaper tomorrow. And then we had a rehearsal, for tomorrow. I had to get up on this huge horse. I was sitting there, and that's when I knew for sure. I think I'd known it all along really. The truth is, it's never been right. Me winning, I mean. Me being chosen as Joan. You wrote the best essay. You should have won. They only chose me because I was born here. Joan wasn't born here, was she? It's not where you're born that counts, is it? I was sitting up there and thinking: Eloise should be on this horse. Eloise should be Joan tomorrow, not me.'

I was filled with a sudden stupendous hope. Marie took my hands in hers. 'Listen, I talked to all the other essay finalists, and they all agreed with me. So this afternoon we went to the Headmaster, and we made him agree too. Will you do it? Will you be Joan tomorrow?'

'But don't you mind?' I asked, still incredulous.

Marie smiled. 'Not really. You deserve it more than me. Soon as I read your essay I knew that. You didn't just study her, did you? You got to know her. You got close. And besides, I was getting very nervous about it all. I hate horses. Honestly, I do. They make me sneeze. You can't have Joan of Arc sneezing her way through the streets of Orléans, can you? So, will you do it?'

'Oh, yes,' I cried. 'I'll do it. I'll do it.' And we stood there hugging each other and crying and swaying together under the silver birches.

'I thought you said you'd lost your cat,' she said in my ear. 'Black and white,

wasn't it?'

I turned round. Mimi! Mimi, sleek and silky in the glow of the evening sun, was rubbing herself up against the trunk of a silver birch, her raised tail trembling with joy.

Marie stayed on late that evening to celebrate Mimi's miraculous return. I took her up to my room, pulled my picture of Joan out from the back of the cupboard and showed it to her.

'I've had her all my life,' I told her.

Marie wrinkled her nose at it. 'Not at all how I imagined her,' she said, 'I've always imagined her very different – more human, more like you.'

*   *   *

The armour was too big. I did not care. My bottom was sore from long hours in the saddle. I did not care. The cathedral bells pealed, the flags waved, the bands played, the people cheered. The whole world seemed happy. I laughed in the sun,

and loved every glorious moment of it. I was Joan, Joan triumphant, Joan adored. I was in raptures. Above my head fluttered my standard, Joan's standard. I waited for the moment. I was sure it would come, but when it did it still took me by surprise. There was a ripple of laughter in the crowd and they were pointing up at my standard. I looked up. There he was, Jaquot, perched high on the point of it and singing his happy heart out.

'The sparrow and the saint,' came a voice from somewhere, from everywhere. A voice I knew so well, my voice from the river. 'The sparrow and the saint.'

Author's Note

When, some years ago, I wrote *Arthur, High King of Britain* and then *Robin of Sherwood* I was simply retelling two old legends in my own way. I had little historical truth to take into consideration. With both books, I was seeking to strip away the encrusted layers of countless tellings, which seemed to me to have distorted the legends. I wanted to discover again, if I could, the living people behind the legends, the Arthur and the Robin who might have inspired the legends in the first place.

But Joan of Arc is, of course, more than a legend. George Bernard Shaw wrote of her in the introduction to his play: 'Joan of Arc was born about 1412, burnt for heresy, witchcraft and sorcery in 1431; rehabilitated after a fashion in 1456, designated Venerable in 1904, declared Blessed in 1908; and finally canonized in 1920.'

Joan of Arc lived and died. She breathed the air we breathe. From the transcripts of her trial in 1431 and her retrial in 1456, we know more about her than any other person of her time. From her own lips she speaks to us down the centuries. And we hear her story, too, from eyewitnesses, from those who knew her as a girl, who grew up with her, who fought with her, who watched her die.

Since her death, Joan has been exploited mercilessly. She has been demonized and vilified – Shakespeare himself was among her detractors. She has been politicized, idolized, and sanctified. They made a legend of her, set her on a pedestal. I tried to find the real Joan, the Joan who grew up in Domrémy. I wanted to be near her, to accompany her through her extraordinary life, to make sense of the innumerable historical inconsistencies and contradictions. Who was this peasant girl who heard voices, who, as a mere teenager, began driving the English out of France and then died at the stake for her beliefs, who inspired the French so much that within just a few years of her death, they had driven the English from their soil forever?

Many biographies by learned authors have been written about her. There have been numerous plays and films, too; but in many cases I found the Joan in them too remote or too saintly. I wanted to see her as she must have been, to share her doubts and her joys, her innermost thoughts. So in my book, I have invented a companion for her, a white sparrow who stays with her faithfully all through her life, right to the end. And to reach back into history, I have used the story of a girl of today who grows up with a picture of Joan of Arc in her house, who admires and loves her deeply. Both devices enabled me to come close to Joan and will, I hope, enable my readers to do the same. But I have neither invented nor embroidered the history – though Joan's story is so remarkable, it might very well seem as if I have! And wherever possible I have used Joan's words. I have let her speak for herself.

Michael Morpurgo–April 15, 1998

Author's Acknowledgments

Many sources were used in the writing of this book. But foremost amongst them have been *St Joan* by Bernard Shaw (Penguin), *Jeanne d'Arc* by Vita Sackville West (Folio Society), *The Trial of Joan of Arc* (Folio Society) and *J'ai nom Jeanne la Pucelle* by Régine Pernaud (Collections Découvertes Gallimard). And many people too have helped. In particular Christine Baker at Gallimard, to whom the book is dedicated, Pam and Colin Webb, my publishers at Pavilion, Philippe Barbeau of Orléans, The Jeanne d'Arc Foundation and the City of Orléans... and, of course, the other Michael, Michael Foreman. My thanks to them all.

Mt St Michel

Chinon

Poitiers

ANGLAIS

BOURGUIGNONS

ARMAGNACS
(France "libre")